VOICES IN THE DARK
Pony Talk and Mining Tales

Derek Hollows

ISBN: 978-1-4457-0898-0

Typeset in Garamond and Engravers MT

CONTENTS

ACKNOWLEDGEMENTS

I thank the Lady Elizabeth Finsberg of Fairford, President of the Bevin Boys' Association for her having kindly written a foreword and Warwick H. Taylor, M.B.E. Vice President of the Association for his complementary introduction.

I am also indebted to my supportive family, to my grandson, Michael for his having appraised the script and to all named herein who granted me copyright permission to record their works.

Together, they made "Voices In The Dark" possible and I am extremely grateful to them for their much-valued assistance.

ABOUT THE AUTHOR

The author was born in Warrington and attended Oakwood Avenue Primary School and the Sir Thomas Le Boteler Grammar School.

From 1944 until 1947, he served as a Bevin Boy at the Lyme Colliery, Haydock, Lancs and progressed from underground haulage work to the coal-face where he was a member of a coal-cutting team. Upon demobilisation, he qualified in Secondary education and retired as a headteacher in Trafford.

His previous work entitled "As I Recall, A Bevin Boy's Story", was launched in 2008 and coincided with the 60th anniversary commemoration of the release of the last Bevin Boys.

He is a member of the Bevin Boys Association and the Battle of Britain Historical Society.

FOREWORD

The Lady Finsberg
President of the Bevin Boys' Association

Congratulations on the publication of your memories of the pit ponies and life underground.
Geoffrey had often regaled me with his experiences of sharing

snap, of his pony keeping him company as well as the times he had with other Bevin Boys in the hostel.

After two and a half years, he returned to life above ground and went on to be Member of Parliament for Hampstead for twenty-two years, President of the Council of Europe, Knight of the Realm and held a Baron's seat in the House of Lords.

I am sure there were times when he was talking to President Gorbachev, debating in the Chamber or travelling from south to north Cyprus that he would like to have had a pony alongside him.

Now, the Bevin Boys Association is so active, I am sure that some of the conversations which arise must include stories of both the coalface and landladies as well as tales relating to those four-legged friends.

Best wishes to all you good chaps from your President,
Elizabeth F.

Photograph courtesy Peter French

Lord Finsberg with a pit pony, Trentham Gardens, Stoke on Trent, 5th October 1996.

Sadly, several days after this photograph was taken, Lord Finsberg passed away. He was an ex-Bevin Boy and President of the Bevin Boys' Association, a position which is now held by his wife, the Lady Finsberg.

INTRODUCTION

Warwick Taylor, M.B.E.
Vice-President, Bevin Boys Association

The British have always had an affection for animals and pit ponies were no exception. Those wonderful, perceptive animals not only knew the contents of your snap tin but also had a great sense of impending danger.

Accidents in coalmines during the 1940's and 1950's are recorded as a death every six hours and a serious accident every two minutes.

One might therefore, ask how many other fatalities and serious accidents could have resulted had it not been for the sixth sense of our dear friend, the pit pony, warning us of dangers that lay ahead.

My colliery in South Wales was converted to modern haulage and conveyor systems whereby ponies were employed only on the surface for the movement of drams.

As I recall, working in South Wales, we Bevin Boys experienced difficulty in getting ponies to obey our commands as we could not speak any of the Welsh language, much to the amusement of the regular miners. Many of those intelligent animals never saw daylight and remained in underground stables for the rest of their lives.

Others only came up to the surface during one week's annual holiday period and when adjusted to the daylight, simply went wild when released into a field. It was not known how many animals were working in the mines during the war but when the industry was nationalized in January, 1947, over 21,000 pit ponies were recorded as coming under the control of the National Coal Board.

This is their story and of those young Bevin Boys and miners who worked with them.

Photograph courtesy of Peter French, B.B.A.

Dan Duhig, Dennis Fisher (Banner Bearer) , Warwick Taylor, M.B.E. Unveiling of plaque in honour of Bevin Boys who served in the Durham and North-East Coalfields. Durham Miners' Hall, Redhill, Durham, 10th July, 2004.

NIL DESPERANDUM

The 11th November, 1989, marked the inception of the Bevin Boys Association. Young men whose uniforms consisted of helmets, safety-boots and protective clothing and whose weapons were picks and shovels, daily risked their lives to win the coal, so vital to the War effort. For far too long, their contribution had been disregarded.

Membership of the Association grew from strength to strength and thanks to the tenacious efforts of various officials with Warwick Taylor playing a key role, recognition for the Bevin Boys was finally granted.

One can well imagine what might have happened had those young men not served King and Country so effectively.

Now, in their twilight years, our comrades' sense of pride in what they achieved at a critical time in our history, has been fully restored.

BUT YESTERYEAR

From early times, horses have been a vital aid to man's livelihood. At least those employed in agriculture enjoyed the light of day, albeit they were hard worked but in the late nineteenth century when the Industrial Revolution was at its height, more than 200,000 horses and ponies slaved in the mines of Britain.

They were considered to be an essential part of the project. Most ponies came from various parts of the United Kingdom but should there be a shortfall in the 10,000 or so annually required to continue the work, they were brought in from European countries and from the U.S.A.

It is sad to relate that they died in their hundreds due to accidents, explosions and most deplorably, mistreatment.

Usually, horses working in shaft mines remained underground throughout their lives and only surfaced to be put down.

The Coal Mines Regulation Act of 1887 allowed inspectors to check on the treatment of horses but this was considered to be completely inadequate and there were protests from a number of pressure groups.

In 1911, a Royal Commission report was issued. This was the Pit Ponies' Charter, the first major legislation. There would now be regular inspection of underground stables, daily records were to be kept, a competent keeper was required to tend every fifteen horses and they were not to work underground until they were four years' old. Leather headgear was introduced to minimize the risk of injury. An ex-miner recounted the story of a strong and frisky pony which was in the habit of breaking away from his keeper. He would charge down the track, scattering everyone in his path

He would then lower his head and ram open the air-door and the miners on the other side would cling tightly to the rock walls in abject fear

The pony later became a model of good behaviour but the doubts that his previous unpredictability aroused, prompted his keeper to design a sturdy, metal helmet which his charge proudly wore for many years.

Sir Robert Gower, President of the Pit Ponies' Protection Society from 1927 until 1951, brought many welfare matters to the Government's attention. Further legislation in 1949 and 1956 made conditions even better.

As the ponies were retired, the National Coal Board and the R.S.P.C.A. undertook the task of re-homing them but there were some who continued to be used in small, private coalmines where there were many infringements of the 1956 regulations.

A quotation from a Royal Commission Report reads: "No one knows how many there are, the hours they work, the lives they lead and the deaths they die" and that observation applied into the 1990's. Even today, it is still not illegal to use horses and ponies underground.

It was only through the introduction and development of mechanisation that their numbers dwindled but salvation came too late for thousands.

We should all remember with deep gratitude the countless number of pit horses and ponies who perished.

They helped make our country great but in so doing, paid a very heavy price.

PONY DRIVERS

TIS A DREAM

Think how it would be to spend your days
In a darkened world, in a perilous maze
Dust enshrouded in a stifling hole,
Suffering, dying, to win the coal.

We crave release from this choking mesh,
To run through pastures, green and fresh
And breathe in air, so clean, so pure:
Yet alas, this life we must endure.

We too, would love to see the sky
But once, dear friends, before we die.
There must be those who hear our plea.
If all are equal, how can this be?

One day, we shall find our sweet release,
When we are blessed by God's great Peace.
Then we will see those pastures green,
In that world of love, a world serene.

D. Hollows

COMPASSION

The majority of miners were passionate animal lovers and they regarded the employment of those noble creatures underground an imposed and necessary evil. They too, were entrapped in an unnatural system which demanded maximum effort by both man and horse.

Their very livelihoods and indeed, the survival of their families depended upon their output and the animals were key players.

Together, they were vital elements in the structure of mining communities. Most of those who worked with ponies forged strong bonds with their charges and treated them with great kindness. Often, my conversations with ex-miners indicate that they considered it a privilege to undertake duties in the company of such hard-working animals and as memories have come flooding back, I have noted feelings of deep grief.

There were many occasions when the instincts of the ponies and horses saved miners from premature death. It was not uncommon for an animal to stop in his tracks and refuse to proceed further down the track, in spite of his handler's prompting.

This usually gave warning of an imminent fall of rock. Similarly, men lost their lives attempting to rescue their pony friends. One of many recorded incidents tells of a fierce fire that raged underground.

Upon hearing of this, a courageous young miner dashed from his home and went below to release the ponies. Tragically, he was overcome by noxious fumes which filled the workings and perished. There isn't any doubting the fact that to incarcerate innocent creatures, some of whom never saw daylight again, was an abomination and an injustice.

A PONY NAMED OXFORD

Doug Williams
Nantmelyn Colliery, Cwmdare, Aberdare, Mid Glamorgan

During my time as a Bevin Boy, I had been working for two years as a surface worker and four years underground. At the time of the incident, I was eighteen years of age and employed as an underground clerk (Measuring Boy) at Nantmelyn Colliery, Cwmdare, Aberdare in Mid-Glamorgan.

One day, the haulier was not in work as he was sick and the overman asked me if I would take the horse, Oxford (who was a light-brown Dartmoor pony), on to the face which was about one mile from the pit bottom. Previously, I had worked with Oxford transporting timber supplies to colliers working at the face and it was normal practice for the horse to be taken back to the stables at the pit bottom about one hour before the end of the shift. At the pit bottom, there was a huge haulage which pulled trams from the double parting.

On this particular day, I knocked nine bells on the wire to alert the haulage man that I was on the way back to the stables with the horse. When we were about one third of the way, the steel rope started to move. It was quite safe at this point in the roadway because the rope was running along the bottom. Quite suddenly, Oxford stopped. The rope was still moving but he would not go on. He stood there shaking. I coaxed and coaxed him to move forward but he would not budge. This was very unusual behaviour for this horse as he was normally a quiet, well-behaved animal. I was about to ring back to the pit bottom to tell the haulage man to stop because the horse would not move when there was a flash, like lightning at my feet and a terrific noise of a whirring sound on either side of me. The steel rope had broken at my feet.

There was such a violent force from this steel rope re-coiling that it had knocked out a number of rings and supporting timbers in front and behind us. After the dust had settled, Oxford went forward without being asked.

Men came running from the pit bottom and were amazed to hear what had happened and how we had escaped from being shredded by the rope. I finished my shift and it was only later that I realised how much danger we had been in and how Oxford had undoubtedly saved my life. I am glad to know that ponies no longer work in the pits.

PIT PONY

Mr. F. Maguire
**Marley Hill Colliery and No.6 Area Black Burn Drift, N.W.
Durham**

Both mines are now long gone. I send a poetic tribute to those
poor animals which I wrote in October, 2001.

FROM HELL TO HEAVEN

On the day I was born,
I heard someone say,
"He will not see much sun
For he is such a little one."

After a few short, happy years,
They sent me to work, to sweat and toil
Way down deep beneath the soil.

After many long years of misery,
My body is aching, my heart is breaking:
My eyes are dim. I can hardly see.

My life is almost over. Soon I will be free.
Heaven may be full but there is a
Place reserved for me.
For I have served my time in Hell.

I am a PIT PONY

In memory of all the poor beasts who never had a real life.

THE LAST PIT PONY AT MARLEY HILL COLLIERY, COUNTY DURHAM

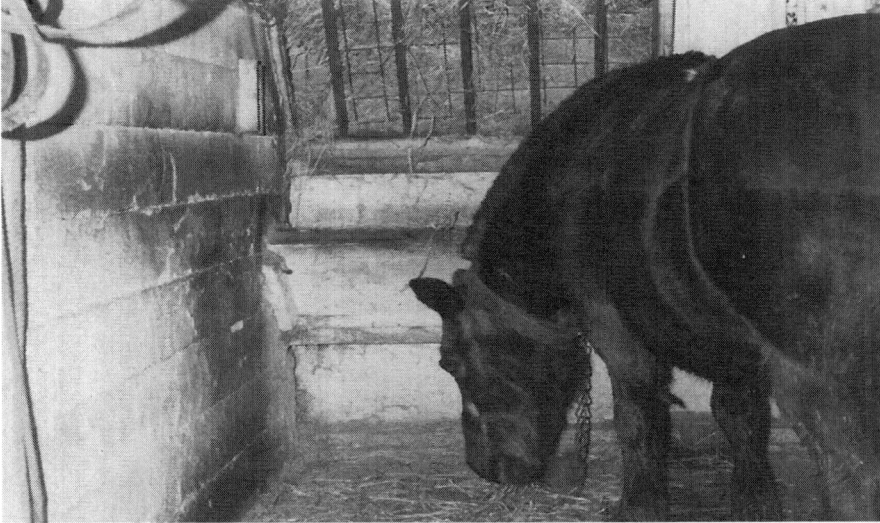

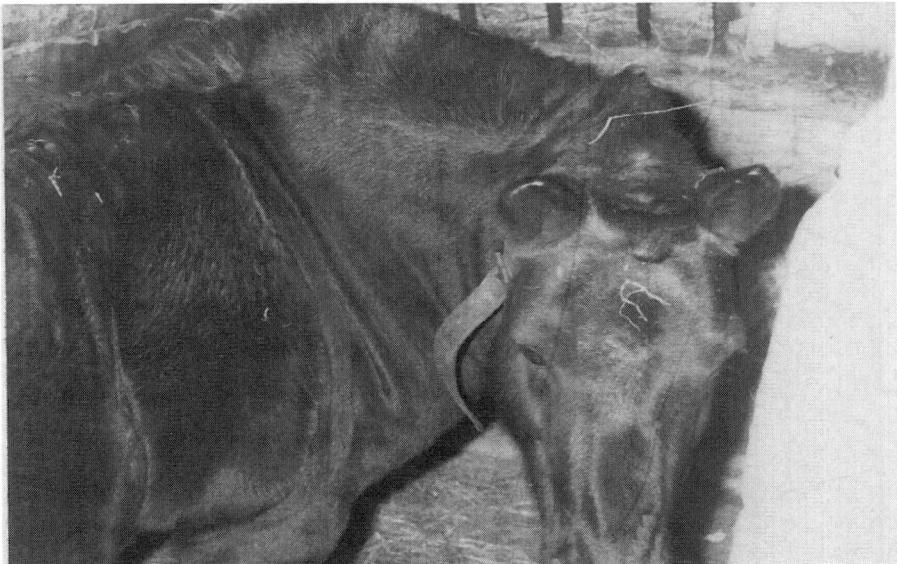

Photographs courtesy Gerry Ash

OFF THE WAY: A NOT INFREQUENT INCIDENT

It was not unknown for canny pit ponies to cause deliberate derailment of tubs. This would afford them a little relaxation before they continued on their way.

DIVERSION

Alan Westmorland
South Pelaw Colliery, Chester-le-Street, Co. Durham

While working in the colliery office as clerk to the manager, I had lunch in the canteen. During one of those breaks, a pit pony which was used in the yard to move pit tubs brought to the surface, caused a not to be forgotten incident. The canteen was quite small, having only six tables and you entered through two swing doors. I was enjoying a leisurely meal when the doors were violently opened. I looked up and there stood the pony with the limbers still attached to its hindquarters. It seems that the pony had been driven through the doors by a person or persons unknown.

Chaos in the canteen was immediate. The limbers were at table level, resulting in dishes and dinners being spattered and crashing to the floor. To make matters worse, the pony lost its balance on the tiled floor. Everyone was in a state of panic, trying to avoid the mess but we were concerned that the pony might hurt itself. Eventually, we managed to get hold of it and take it outside, none the worse for wear. Needless to say, no one had lunch that day as most of the food was scattered all over the floor.

It was obvious that the pony had been guided through the canteen doors as a prank. In spite of our enquiries, the culprits were never identified. However, no one was hurt during the chaos as most of us, including myself, had taken refuge behind the serving counter.

CAREER PATH

Gerald (Gerry) Ash
Middle Management, N.C.B. Team Valley

My father and both grandfathers were miners and I spent the first twenty-five years of my life living in Tanfield Lea, a mining village in north-west Durham.

Every resident in the area depended on the local colliery for a living but it closed down in 1962.

I recall that as a very young boy, I used to visit the pit pony field in the village centre.

I would stand and admire them and there was always one being spoiled by us as it nibbled the bread and fruit which we offered.

The highlight of the year was the day when all the ponies were brought to the surface at the start of the colliery holidays.

We would watch them getting accustomed to the sunlight and rolling in the grass.

I well remember my mother filling my father's bait box and the first thing that went into it was "Something for Blackie", my father's pony.

According to Dad, Blackie would not move out of the stable until he had finished his treat. During the pre-war years, all the mines were on short-time working. Among them was Pelton Colliery, Chester-le-Street and on the 28th June, 1932, my grandfather, Robert Ashmore Redpath, the undermanager and three of his colleagues were descending to inspect the pit and feed the ponies when the cage jerked downwards and pulled the rope taut. Tragically, three of the men including my grandfather were thrown down the shaft to their deaths. It is little wonder that my father ensured that my three brothers and I should not become miners as four previous generations had been.

On the day I left school in December, 1949, my father asked me what I wanted to do for a living. I quickly replied, "A pit- man like my mates." "Right," he replied "Let us go down to the colliery and I will show you what it is all about."

I must have been thick because only Dad who was an overman and I were underground on Christmas Eve. Dad carried out an inspection and together we fed the ponies. We crawled along some seams that were less than three feet high and surfaced twelve hours later.

"Still want to be a miner?" Dad asked.

"No way," I replied but in January, 1950, I did the next best thing. I started work as an office boy at the National Coal Board headquarters in Newcastle-upon-Tyne where I earned the princely sum of £1.18d per week.

When mines began to close down, one of my jobs was to dispose of office equipment.

There was a surplus of pit ponies in the Durham area and the pit pony stables at Leadgate were no longer used.

I found a good home for a retired pony on a farm where my brother was the manager.

I recall walking into the empty stables at Leadgate and I saw a framed copy of a poem which was hanging in a prominent place. It was entitled "The Prayer of a Horse" and I learned that it had been written in 1915 by a lady called Edith Cole.

She was an actress and authoress, living in Birkenhead. She also wrote a book, "Scarlet and Grey" and all proceeds were donated to the Blue Cross Fund to help wounded horses in the front line during World War One.

THE PRAYER OF A HORSE.

To thee, my master, I offer my prayer:

"Feed me with food clear of dust and well mixed with bran and oats, also water and care for me, and when the day's work is done provide me with shelter, a clean dry bed, and a stall wide enough for me to lie down in comfort. Talk to me. Your voice often means as much to me as the reins. Pet me sometimes, that I may serve you the more gladly and learn to love you. Do not jerk the reins, and do not whip me when going up hill. Never strike, beat or kick me when I do not understand what you mean, but give me a chance to understand you. Watch me, and if I fail to do your bidding see if something is not wrong with my harness or feet.

Examine my teeth when I do not eat. I may have an ulcerated tooth, and that, you know, is very painful. Do not tie my head in an unnatural position or take away my best defence against flies and mosquitoes by cutting off my tail.

And finally, oh! my master, when my useful strength is gone do not turn me out to starve or freeze or sell me to some cruel owner, to be slowly tortured and starved to death; but do thou, my master, take my life in the kindest way and your God will reward you here and hereafter.

You may not consider me irreverent if I ask this in the name of Him who was born in a stable."—*Amen.*

DONNA AND MIDDY

Susan Potts
Gerald Ash's niece

In the sixties, my mother and father agreed to let me have a pony as we had moved to a farm in Cumbria and therefore had access to fields and stables. I was about five years of age and loved horses. The wife of my father's boss, Mrs. Johnson by name, already had her thoroughbred, Donna, in a field just next to our house and they gave us permission to put a pony in with her.

We had heard that there was a farm in County Durham where they were looking for good homes for retired pit ponies and thought this was a very good idea, especially so as my grandfather had worked down the mines for most of his life in the area. We therefore arranged to visit the farm in Consett for an interview and to view the ponies.

I cannot recall if he had been broken-in to ride but seem to remember that we had to arrange training later. I struggled to decide especially between two Shetlands which were available for they were just about the right size for me.

In the end, I went for a stumpy-legged, well-rounded dark pony called Middy who was nearly as wide as he was hands high. I got a nice new saddle and bridle which I looked after well with special saddle soap plus brushes and combs to groom my new pet.

Middy settled in very well at Easby Farm, making immediate friends with Donna who seemed to treat him as if he were her foal. He could actually walk under her stomach.

They were inseparable, neighing and whinnying at each other whenever I took Middy out of the field either to groom him or for a ride up the road.

I could never go very far because Middy would just stop and not go any further or he would even turn round of his own accord and head back to Donna. He was a very placid, contented and sometimes, lazy pony really.

Several years later, we had to move from the farm but I continued to visit Middy as often as I could. Sadly, the day came when my father rang me to say that he had arrived at work only to find Middy dead in the field and it seemed that old age had taken its toll. I know only too well that Middy enjoyed a restful retirement and lived out his latter years happily with his great friend and companion, Donna.

SAM

Alfred Gaddas
Dean and Chapter Colliery, Ferryhill, Co. Durham

As a Bevin Boy between 1945 and 1948, most of my time was spent working with pit ponies. This was probably because as a farmer's son from Westmorland, I was used to working with horses and other animals.

Dean and Chapter Colliery had over 300 ponies working below ground when I was there.

Following initial training at Anfield Plain, my first day at Ferryhill was spent taking props and planks to a long-wall face. Our route was from the main engine plain via the tailgate, which was so low that we used the smallest ponies in the pit to pull the trams laden with timber to the working coalface. The tailgate was so long that the pony and I could only manage two loads per shift.

At other times, I was putting tubs with a pony. This involved taking empties to a loader head and when filled, transferring them to the pit bottom so that they could be sent to the surface. In one area, the ponies were up to their bellies in water. We too, got wet but received five shillings extra per week for working in water. It was in that wet area that I received a bonus. In the rock above me, I saw the fossilized remains of thousands of beautiful palm fronds. This inspired a new interest for me, namely Geology, which has fascinated me to the present day.

The last eighteen months or so of my service down the mine again involved my taking props and planks to the coalface.

This time, the route was alongside the conveyor belt which was our most modern piece of machinery at the time. There was insufficient space for a rail track to run the timber train so the pony had to drag six props or planks with a trace chain wrapped around them to the face. From there, I would untie the chain and manhandle them the rest of the way.

My pony was called 'Sam', a white Shetland and so small that had I sat astride him, I would have been able to touch the ground with the toe of my boot. Sam was no ordinary pony, a fact which he demonstrated on many occasions but we were involved in two incidents that proved he was extra-ordinary.

One day, as he was dragging his load of timber beside the conveyor-belt, he suddenly stopped. After telling him to "Go on" a few times, I noticed that although the belt was running, it was empty. Ahead of us, a very large chunk of coal had come up against a low girder and was stuck. This had caused all the following coal to plough off the belt, blocking our path.

To no avail, Sam was scraping at it with his hoof. I rang to stop the conveyor, then climbed over it to the other side and crawled along past Sam and the pile of coal. Having removed the large lump from between the girder and the belt, I restarted the belt and proceeded to put the coal back on with my bare hands. Meanwhile, Sam was doing his best to help me by digging with his feet through the pile of coal from the other side. Before I had managed to clear it all, he was down on his knees, attempting to work his way through to me, despite my asking him to "Wait" until I had cleared more coal. At a later date, not long before I was demobbed, Sam showed just how intelligent he really was. A conveyor-belt can only run in a straight line.

However, the arch girders that were forming the 'main gate' where we were working were not parallel with the belt.

Consequently, there was much less room for Sam to turn round after I had untied the trace-chain at the coalface. The space grew more and more narrow as new girders were put in place. One day, it was so bad that when I called to Sam "Come round", he could not manage to do so. After a few attempts, he looked at me as if to say, "You must be joking, surely?"

Finally, after several more attempts to turn, he placed his front feet on to the belt, allowing the conveyor to carry his body round. He, then calmly stepped down just as if he had done it every day of his life, or been trained in a circus.

WHAT GOES ROUND, COMES ROUND

During my researches, I was not surprised to learn that over the years, there have been recorded cases of extreme cruelty inflicted on horses and ponies who laboured in the mines. In certain instances, special whips and even electric shocks were used on uncooperative animals. When reported, such malpractices could be punished by termination of one's employment, temporary suspension from duty, removal of all further contact with the ponies or physical punishment of offenders by their work colleagues. The adage, 'A man without a conscience is far more dangerous than any beast' cannot be disputed.

An ex-collier from the County Durham Coalfield recounted his story thus:

"Referring to behaviour underground and for obvious reasons, mining regulations prohibited smoking, the consumption of alcohol, sleeping whilst on duty and fighting. My workmates and I were infuriated by the ill-treatment of a certain pony by his handler and I was chosen to deal with the matter. At the end of the shift, I approached him in the pit-yard and after advising him of the reason for the confrontation, gave him the hiding of his life. He begged for mercy as cowards are wont to do and staggered off, homeward bound.

He did not turn up for work the next day and we later learned that he had left the mine and the local area in great haste for he knew only too well that there were others ready and willing to mete out justice in like manner. So much for the courage of bullies."

JUST DESSERTS

A creature abused in a darkened mine.
"Mind thy own business, this pony ain't thine.
'Treat 'im kinder', I 'eard thee say.
Well, I'll do me job in me own special way."

Compassionate miners know it's not right
To witness this deed, a pitiful sight;
So knuckles whiten and hackles rise
But the bully ignores the animal's cries.

Shift's ended and abuser strides above,
Devoid of conscience, emptied of love.
He stops, confronted by a grimy face
And fearful, quickens his ambling pace.

"Want summat, do yer?" - an anxious shout
A clenched fist responds: slap, bang on his snout.
"Gie o'er, it 'urts. I'm feelin' reet sick"
Then a passing pony gives him a kick.

"I'll change me ways, I ave no fear",
He moans atop the winding-gear.
A lesson learned? There is no doubt
Accrediting all to a kick and a clout.

"Seen t'bully today?" comes a miner's cry.
Nay, but las' neet 'e were all but in t'sky."
"Well, tha can tell 'im 'e's just had t'sack."
"No need, owd lad, t'b****r won't be back."

D. Hollows

FAREWELL DARKNESS

THE VIEWING PARTY

FRESH AIR AT LAST

A JOB WELL DONE

J.A. Taylor, Little Lever, Bolton
The photographs are of pit ponies returning to the surface at the Ladyshore
Colliery, in Little Lever. The mine closed down many years ago.

THROUGH MY EYES

"Not bad considering his age. A few breathing problems. I recommend retirement," I overheard the vet remark. And so it was. Gently coaxed and with head enshrouded in sacking soon to be removed and discarded, I emerge from the cage and tentatively step forward. Slowly, my eyes adjust to the daylight.

It is then that I experience a gamut of mixed emotions with sheer joy nullifying my trepidation. Before me, stands a small assembly of mine-workers who welcome me to the surface.

Patted, stroked and praised, I am filled with ecstasy and eager anticipation and become immersed in the pleasures of celebrity status. Holding myself erect with pride, I gaze in awe at the vast expanse of a world bathed in dazzling sunlight, a world that was denied me so many years ago. That benevolent heavenly body sheds its comforting rays over me and deeply, I inhale the sweet, fresh air, the elixir of life.

"Can this be true?" I question "Or is it merely a repetition of the recurrent dream that I experienced throughout those long years deep underground?"

Roddie, the ostler's assistant, leads me to the stable where I am washed, groomed, fed and watered. With gentle touch, he applies soothing oils to my lacerated back and then escorts me to an adjoining field.

As he gives me a tender hug, he whispers, "Well done, owd lad. Tha's free at last. I'll come an' see thee every day wi' some treats." A final pat and with tears in his eyes, he turns, secures the gate and disappears toward the pit-head.

Now I stand alone. I am so accustomed to following instructions that I feel lost and vulnerable. With heavy heart, I recall those men and ponies who perished in the stifling darkness.

As with men at war, I am plagued by the guilt of survival. For a fleeting moment, I wish myself back among my friends. I am missing them already and especially my soul-mate, Blackie, the Shetland. He was my constant companion and we shared so much together during those days of enslavement. I know that he would lighten my remorse by counselling me to enjoy my well-earned liberty.

On that note, I stomp, snort and whinny and charge across the pastures toward a distant fence. I stop and breathe heavily for I have not escaped the legacy of dust-laden air but I am overjoyed now that I have entered the realm of divine release.

In my solitude, I know that many of my kind have preceded me into that same meadow.

I let my thoughts wander. Could it be that I am surrounded by a host of kindly spirits? Anything is possible. I have a strong feeling that thoughts projected from an ethereal world impinge on my consciousness and I voice them aloud: 'Time to let go', 'The past is over 'Enjoy God's gifts' and as if touched by a healing hand, my turbulent thoughts are becalmed and again, I become aware of the lush carpet beneath my feet.

With the setting of the sun, comes a cooling breeze and transient shadows sweep the ground. A loud squawking from above attracts my attention. I espy a flock of birds soaring overhead, undoubtedly homeward bound. As they crest the currents, I can only admire their courage and tenacity, in spite of their frailty. Their lives too, are committed to survival and they persevere despite the perils that beset them. I know that for a few moments, I am in good company for they display traits that I witnessed in the mine.

Suddenly, my reverie is disturbed by a firm but friendly nudge. Startled, I turn and am overcome by euphoria for standing by my side is my chum, Blackie. Reunited at last, our loud whinnies of excitement echo across the field. I can only pray that the sound of our mutual happiness will resonate through those dark workings, giving hope to all our friends that one day, they may be blessed as Blackie and I are, to share their twilight years in God's green pastures.

D. Hollows

BITTER SWEET MEMORIES (EXTRACTS)

Dennis Fisher
Ex-Bevin Boy and miner who served for twenty years in the County Durham Coalfield (Chilton Colliery)

Most of the collieries in our part of the county had very little mechanized coal-cutting machinery. Most of the coal was hard won by the hewers using compressed-air-hand picks and all the tubs were filled by hand with large pan shovels, the size of which would make any ordinary man weep. The empty tubs were taken to the coalface by ponies. Their handlers called putters, were on piece-work and paid by the score.

The coal seams didn't all run straight and level but went up steep, high sides and steep dips which would really tax a pony's strength.

A lot of the workings were in wet, terrible conditions. We were breathing in fumes from the explosives used by the coal hewers which hung about the workings for hours. Sometimes, we worked through black damp gas which floated just above the floor and the air's oxygen content was so low that the oil lamps' flames were almost nil.

After a hard-worked shift, the coal hewers came out with thumping headaches.

With every working shift, the old "Death Reaper" was never far away and if he swept forward his scythe, he never pushed aside any favourites. All were cut down, face workers, Bevin Boys and pit ponies alike. My pit had many fatal casualties, all good workers. Some were my friends and I still remember them all. Who could forget?

The ponies never complained. Maybe there was nobody to hear them.

After all, they had no choice.

At the pit where I worked there were two hundred of these little animals stabled underground.

All their lives they never saw daylight.

Without the ponies, the pit's targets would never have been reached. A commemorative statue should be erected to those thousands of gallant, little animals - and to the Bevin Boys. Without them, the fight for coal for the war effort would never have been won.

This compilation of extracts from "Bitter Sweet Memories" is reproduced by kind permission of the author, Dennis Fisher and first appeared under the title "Pride Before the Fall" in "Bands and Banners" magazine, Autumn/Winter edition, 2000/2001.

SWALLOW

When first I went underground to serve King and Country, I felt very honoured when I was sent to work in the stables to replace a horse-keeper who was sick. Chilton Colliery had two stables and without those ponies there wouldn't have been any coal produced. There was a pony hospital on the surface which was clean and quiet.

It was warm in the stables and there were a number of dim electric lights. Most Bevin Boys started working at the bottom of the shaft which was really cold during the winter months. Even so, the majority were quite happy and had no intention of moving further in-bye to work nearer the coalface.

All I can say is that they missed out on a lot as it was an education which helped us grow up into men.

Working in the stables, I got to know every one of the ponies. I took notice of everything that the experienced horse-keepers told me. One piece of advice was that if my oil-lamp were to be accidentally extinguished and if I were cast into complete darkness, I must grab hold of the straps on the pony's gears and he would lead me to the safety of the shaft bottom. I was also told that if the pony stopped and would not travel further, I must be wary for he would be trying to warn me that there was danger ahead.

I learned a lot from one old horse-keeper who managed to prepare a hot, steaming tin of soup for his bait. There weren't any kettles, cookers or canteen ladies and I wondered how he was able to do it. One day, I watched him.

He punched a hole in the top of the tin and then scratched out a hole in a tub of horse manure and carefully placed the tin into the hole. Within minutes, he had a red-hot tin of steaming soup.

When I started pony putting, I was on piece-work and took the empty tubs to the hewers and brought out the full tubs. All this was done by pony power.

I worked with a pony called Swallow. I will always remember an incident involving the two of us. We were working on the foreshift, in the middle of the night and drawing tubs to and from Ray, a hewer. Ray had been a survivor of Dunkirk. I saw that Swallow was catching his back on the plank supports where Ray was working. It seemed strange for there hadn't been a problem when we started. I shouted to Ray to tell him that the main roadway was sealing up. Swallow would not move. The prop supports were sinking into the floor. Then the roof collapsed. Luckily, Ray had already moved from his working area but Swallow and I were trapped on the coalface which was the safest place to be during a roof-fall. It was impossible to get Swallow out so I took him out of the tub limbers and used them to support the roof and then stripped him of his harness which I placed on a full tub of coal. I managed to slither out through the old workings that weren't completely sealed. I made my way to the stables and reported that Swallow was trapped by a fall.

I told the manager and head horse-keeper how I had escaped and it was decided that a fresh roadway should be driven through the old workings, enabling the keeper to reach Swallow and feed him. My father was one of those who helped. It took two weeks to reach the pony. Work started on a new roadway high enough to get Swallow out which took two months. At last, he was freed but naturally, he had lost weight.

One day, the old horse-keeper from whom I had learned so much, approached me and patted me on the back "Well done, lad," he said. "The best thing you did for that pony was taking off his head-piece and all his harness." Because of that action, Swallow was able to feed himself by chewing the bark from the timber roof supports and this had helped keep him alive until contact with the keeper was made. Although I was six feet in height, the old horse-keeper's compliment made me feel seven feet tall.

D. Fisher

CHEEKY COCKNEY BEVIN BOY

We had a fair number of Bevin Boys at Chilton Colliery who came from London and the Southern region. One cheeky Cockney who wouldn't move from his job at the bottom of the shaft made all the lads laugh. He was stopped one day by the overman who said to him, "I want you to go to the stables and report to the horse-keeper. Tell him that you want to take a pony to Carrington's Flat on the East side of the Old Main Coal. He will show you which one and you will put on his harness gears. The pony will show you the way."
The Cockney looked the overman straight in the eye and replied, "Look, mate, I'm a b**** y Bevin Boy, not a b****y cowboy."
He didn't even enter the stables let alone lead the pony to where it was needed. After that flat refusal, the job was assigned to someone else - Yours truly, Joe Soap.

'Kit', a First Prize winning pony out of Chilton Colliery stables with Horse-Keeper, Billy Local. You could find no better working pony than Kit. I swear that he fully understood English and was almost human.

D. Fisher

HEE-HAW

A lot of ponies destined to work in our mines came from America. They were purchased under contract in allocations of a thousand at a time.

On one occasion, a mule was sent to make up the number agreed. The ponies were shipped by sea to Liverpool Docks and then by rail to County Durham. Finally, they were transported by road to a distribution centre in the small township of Willington.

From there, they were sent to the various collieries. We were surprised to see a mule arrive at Chilton Colliery where it would be broken-in by Bert Wardell, the trainer who had a magic touch with new, unbroken ponies.

Chilton's mule had a very large, bony head and long ears that stuck forward.

It also had another distinctive feature which I did not know about until I was sent to feed him in his stall. I was accustomed to hearing quiet whinnies from the other ponies in the stable.

On that particular day, I stood close to his muzzle as I fed him, too close in fact. Suddenly, he lifted his head, rolled back his top lip and he brayed loudly in my ear. In the silence of the stables, it sounded louder than ever. I nearly jumped out of my skin with fright.

After that, he became known as Hee Haw, a name which was to stick with him. While waiting for a year to become a pony putter, I compiled a list of the pit ponies' names and their temperaments. Hee Haw was listed among the " good uns". Sadly, I never got to work with Hee Haw for I am sure, that we would have made a great working-team.

D. Fisher

SIMON

The men would hear him coming and as he drew near, they could see in the rays of their cap lamps, his blazing, red eyes and then with mouth wide open, he would show his flashing teeth. Without hesitation, the miners would scatter, with some jumping on top of the tubs of coal and others diving into the safety refuges built into the rock wall.

Simon, a grey, wouldn't stop until he reached the cages. Then he would turn round and repeat the charge, forcing the men to flee a second time.

He never failed to do this at the end of his working shift until he became old and his energy was spent. No longer was he able to do his party-trick.

Of all the ponies in the stable, Simon will long be remembered by the pitmen who would cross themselves as he charged toward them. After his performances were completed, he would turn into the stables for his 'choppy' and oats. It is small wonder that Desert Orchid, another grey, won the Grand National.

D. Fisher

SPAM

During World War Two, a very acceptable gift came from the U.S.A. in the shape of tins of Spam. It certainly helped supplement our meagre meat ration. There were also tins of powered dried eggs which when mixed and fried, turned into a type of utility rubber, ideal for repairing car tyres but it helped assuage our hunger. When my mother got hold of her first tin of Spam, she held it aloft and ran round the kitchen table in excitement. One would have thought that she had just won the World Cup.

The next morning, I returned home from the night shift and she asked if I had enjoyed my Spam sandwiches. I replied, "They were very nice, thanks." Certainly, it made a welcome change from strawberry teacakes minus the butter.

Here I give you a word of warning. Never tell your mother or your wife that you have enjoyed Spam sandwiches or you'll be eating them until they come out of your ears. I speak from long-suffering experience for from that day forward, it was Spam, Spam, Spam and more Spam.

Mind you, I must admit that the pit ponies really loved it. When I married, my mother said to my new bride, "He's very partial to Spam in his bait" and sure enough that is what I got day in, day out.

In desperation, I asked my wife for a change of diet and that is exactly what I got. The Spam was now sprinkled with tomato ketchup and the ponies loved it even more. Eventually, I had to tell my wife that she was wasting time and money for the ponies were eating the lot. However, I made a point of saving my bread crusts for them.

Pit ponies will eat just about anything and everything, even the paper wrappings from your bait. I've known them to enjoy a treat of orange peel and I once worked with a pony who would not budge until he was given a chew of my baccy.

I remember with deep affection the bravery of the hard-working pit ponies who spent their lives working in low seams. They were clever little pets and the miners were very attached to them. They got up to tricks that made circus ponies look like amateurs. I still recall seeing them copying the miners at the end of a shift, perching on the conveyor belts. They presented a comical sight as they bounced quite unconcerned over the tops of the rollers.

D. Fisher

BARSON

Bill Bolton
Dawdon Colliery, Co. Durham

I spent six years at Dawdon Colliery and for most of that time, I worked with pit ponies.

One of my jobs was pony drawing from a landing to the putters' flat up a short incline. With me sitting on the limbers, the pony would then draw the three nine-hundredweight tubs down the slope.

During one shift, the pony lost its footing and fell on the side where I was sitting. My lamp was extinguished and I was in total darkness. I was trapped for quite some time but eventually managed to free myself. I considered myself extremely lucky for the limbers could have severed my leg. Instead, I had a very badly bruised knee which kept me off work for some weeks.

I am glad to say that my pony, Barson, was as right as rain and continued to carry out his duties as if nothing had happened.

He was a lovely friend and companion.

TITCH, FOREVER LOVED AND NEVER FORGOTTEN

When I was learning the ropes, one of the ponies was called Titch. He was a Shetland and so small that when I stood on tiptoe, he could walk between my legs with ease.

He was not allowed to go out with the putters because he was tiny and he was used wholly for work in the stables where he would pull one empty tub at a time which was filled with manure from the stalls. He also pulled a tub laden with 'choppy' (hay) and bags of crushed oats to feed the other ponies.

Some collieries had 'pit yackers', men who liked to invite trouble which often developed into bare-fist fighting. They would fight on their way to work, on their way home and even in the pit-yard before going on shift.

Among them, were those who would flex their muscles and show off their strength to intimidate their opponents by lifting Titch's rear end off the ground but if I caught them at it, I would give them a warning and if it went unheeded, I would take further action.

In those days, I too, packed a hefty punch which the offenders knew about to their peril.

Titch was much loved by the miners and on show days, was led to bank to enjoy the fresh air and daylight. At these shows, he won a number of prizes. But Titch was getting on in years and when word got round that the N.C.B. area vet, was doing his pony check-ups, Titch was moved out of the stables and hidden away.

Very soon, the vet became aware of this. It became obvious that due to his advanced years, Titch was going to be put down. Many pit-men offered to buy him from the N.C.B.

Even the colliery manager expressed a wish to give him a new home so that he might enjoy his remaining years on the surface. Sadly, the laws of the mine beat them all. It was a very moving and emotional time for those who had loved that beautiful little Shetland pony.

During his lifetime, he had brought so much happiness and peace to all who were privileged to know him.

D. Fisher

Photograph courtesy of D. Fisher

TITCH

TOT

Derek Gillum
Silksworth, Seaham and Vanetempest Collieries

I worked with pit ponies at Silksworth Colliery. I would get up at 2.30a.m. and set off for the pit at 3.00a.m. which was three miles from my home. I would then go down in the cage and make my way to the Hutton stables where the ponies were housed.

The first shift would start at 4.00a.m. and I made sure that I was underground ten minutes before the men arrived. My pony, Tot, was very small and coloured black. Together, we would walk the two miles to the workings where we drew the trams. At our mine in the 1960's and 1970's, ponies were only used to take timber to the coalface or to pull out tubs.

I was eighteen years of age when I started working with them and I loved every minute. It was a privilege to have them as companions.

In all, I spent twenty-five years in the mines.

Derek is a talented author and has produced a number of works based on the mining theme.

MORE TOT

Peter Shields
Silksworth and Wearmouth Collieries (1966-1992), Hon.
Secretary, Silksworth Banner Group

When the mines were opened in Northern England, the pit ponies came from Galloway in Scotland and were known as 'Gallowas'. The last of the surviving ponies finished work in the 1990's. I started work at Silksworth Colliery in 1966 and was employed as a fitter's apprentice. Although I did not work with the ponies, I often came into contact with them as they were used to carry machinery and timber to us.

I well remember a pony called 'Tot' who worked in the South East Hutton Seam.

If Tot saw you taking a pinch of snuff, he would stand next to you and give you a nudge. He too, wanted his share so you put a pinch up his nostril and quickly moved out of the way because when he sneezed, you could find yourself covered in all sorts of things. As if that wasn't enough, he would wait for you to put a pinch up his other nostril. Obviously he appreciated the therapeutic value of the powdered tobacco. Probably, it cleared his nostrils of all the dust that he had inhaled during the course of his work.

There was also another pony who was in the habit of jumping on the man-riding belt at the end of the shift. No more legwork for him that day and they always say "If you can't beat 'em, join 'em".

HIGHWAY ROBBERY

"Reckon us 'as got a thief down 'ere," said Tommy.

"What makes thee think that?" Sammy asked.

"Cos somebody keeps pinchin' me pigtail," came the reply "Been goin' on for weeks now."

"Can't be any of us lads. Miners don't nick owt off one another, Jimbo remarked.

"Course they don't but who the 'ell is it then? Thing is, I ties it to a prop an' when I fancy a chew an' nips off to get it, it just ain't theer. I'm that busy, I can't keep me eye on it all t'time."

"Shove it in thy pocket then," Sammy advised.

"Pocket, what pocket?" came the response.

"It's that 'ot down 'ere, I only wears me clogs an' there's no pockets in me shorts."

"I've been thinkin', could be t'mice, tha knows. Given t'chance, they'll polish off all thy snap. Might fancy a bit o'baccy for puddin' ," suggested Jimbo.

"Only t'other day, I were watchin' one scrabblin' round in t'dust wi' 'is mates an' I could swear 'e 'ad a pipe in 'is chops. Might be 'avin' a crafty smoke," Sammy joked.

"'ang on, I've got an idea," Jimbo proposed. "Can't go wrong, this 'ide thysen near t'prop wi' t'pigtail on it an' 'ave a stick o'chalk 'andy. Then switch off thy leckie an' wait.

When t'thief goes to t'prop, grab 'im an' draw a line reet down 'im , from top to bottom like."

"Tha's a genius, Jimbo," Tommy responded.

The following day, Tommy turned off his lamp and with a piece of chalk in his hand, awaited the arrival of the miscreant.

He was enveloped in total darkness. He was on the point of nodding off but his senses were suddenly sharpened when he heard the sound of approaching steps which grew louder and louder and then stopped immediately opposite him. There came the sound of a slight tapping which came from the area of the prop. In an instant, he lunged forward, pressing the chalk against the invisible form and drew a vertical line. Then he switched on his lamp. "Gotcha," he shouted in triumph but his comment bore little fruit for Turpin, the pit pony, turned and galloped off down the track at full speed, with the pigtail firmly clenched between his teeth.

Based on a true story from the Lancashire Coalfield.

D. Hollows

MINER AND PENNY

George Daughtery
Co. Durham Coalfield

At the age of fourteen years, I left school on the Friday afternoon and started working in the pit the following Monday. I spent fifteen years in the industry and served in various mines in County Durham.

During my early days, I was put in charge of a beautiful Shetland pony called Miner.. He was a bantam with a height of only two feet eight inches. He was so small that we worked in an 18" - 24" seam and Miner was used solely to pull out the coal cutter so that it could be transferred elsewhere.

One day, he and I were travelling along the haulage-way when he suddenly stopped in his tracks. I tapped him gently on the buttocks and tried to coax him to move forward. It was all to no avail. He absolutely refused to budge and I could not understand why. I checked to see if he had injured himself but I could not find anything untoward.

Then it happened. The walls of the road ahead and the roof collapsed. Tons of rock fell, completely sealing the track and I knew that Miner's intuitive senses had saved both our lives. Some time later, I worked with a lovely Welsh pony named

Penny.

When I became a collier, I worked on a low face, so low in fact that I found it impossible to turn over the blade of my shovel. The area in which I worked was not only cold but very damp. I was fortunate in that a close friend of mine owned a nearby field and when the pit closed down, I adopted Miner who spent the last nine years of his life enjoying the freedom of galloping through green pastures.

Sadly, he died at the age of twenty-nine years. I also adopted Penny and she too, was able to enjoy her retirement in the same field. I have always loved animals

I miss my two little friends and I retain very happy memories of them both.

NELSON AND BERT

Ron Holloway
Bestwood Colliery

After working underground for a few months, the under-manager told me to take a pony and work with contractors who were enlarging a roadway. I was given a big, grey pony called 'Nelson' which was nicknamed Nellie.

It was much taller than I and unknown to me at the time, he was full of tricks. The foreman contractor showed me how to couple up the empties and Nellie found it easy to pull them four hundred yards up an incline to the workings. My job was to keep the men supplied with about twenty empty tubs during the shift and remove loaded tubs to the main haulage road.

As we were on an incline, I found that I only needed the pony to bring up the empties. The full tubs would run down to the junction where I could peg them. One day, Nellie started to play his tricks on me. As soon as I tried to hitch him up to the empties, he bolted. I chased him, caught him and tried again with the same result. Finally, I fastened lengths of shot-firing wire to both ends of his bit and held it as though they were reins.

As soon as he heard the chain clink, he started off but I pulled him back with the wires, only to find him circling round me at the junction. A passing group of miners wisecracked that there was a Bevin Boy in the pit who was training ponies for the circus. Even when hitched to tubs Nellie would pull away with a sudden jerk and derail the first tub. Sometimes he used to move sideways and step hard on to my steel-capped boots. My toes became trapped and I had to hammer the toecaps against a rail to release them.

Since then, my toes have been permanently damaged and even today, I have to file the nails which have grown thick to ensure that they don't wear holes through the tops of my shoes.

On another occasion, I was leading him up to the main road. There was a run of empty tubs attached to the haulage rope.
At the same time a train of full tubs came by in the opposite direction. The space between the two runs of tubs was restricted but I thought it would be safe to move forward as the tubs were not touching Nellie's harness. Suddenly, he bolted and knocked me to the ground between the moving tubs. He then jumped over me and disappeared into the darkness. When the tubs had passed and all was quiet again, I could hear his hooves clattering as he galloped at top speed in the direction of the stables. On my way to retrieve him, I had to pass the haulage engine house. The engine man shouted "He went by so fast that I thought he was in the 'Grand National."
In the stables, I reported the incident to the ostler who advised me that on one occasion, Nellie had been trapped between tubs and injured so that whenever he faced a similar situation, he would panic. He added that in narrow spaces, one should turn and face the pony so that the cap lamp would shine in his eyes. Then one should hold both sides of his bit and walk him

backwards into an open space. In view of this information, it is understandable why Nellie panicked.

Later, I worked with Nellie in a wet area. The roof was constantly bitting and the faulty length was reinforced with pit props and girders. A few days afterwards, the roof collapsed, burying all our tubs and it took three months to clear the debris.
Nellie then began to work with another Bevin Boy. He was now much more docile and obedient. He would pull his load to the top of an incline and hold them there without any assistance. Naturally, I asked for an explanation regarding his changed behaviour. I learned that the Bevin Boy's father was in charge of the delivery horses for a London brewery and the lad had been brought up with horses.

There were only five ponies in the Bestwood High Main seam but not one of them was as fiery as Nellie.
Another smaller pony was called Bert who would always come to you when called. He would beg on his hind legs for a sandwich. You can imagine the panic experienced by a new boy when Bert reared up at the sight of his sandwiches.
Bestwood was a highly mechanised pit and in 1942, produced a million tons of coal. The ponies were finally phased out.
Finally, the memories of Nellie remain with me to this day. Several years later, after the boot crushing incident, I would shout out in my sleep "Nellie, get off my foot." My landlady was absolutely convinced that I had a girl friend called Nellie.

BEN, BUD AND JACK

Roy Atkinson
Fleetingly Beck Colliery, Swillington, W. Yorks
Frystone Colliery, near Castleford

I started working at the colliery when I was fourteen years old and my first job involved pulling tubs out of the cage and coupling them up to be sent inbye.

After a few weeks, I was told to go pony-driving which meant that I had to take pit props from the end of the haulage way to the coalface. My pony's name was Ben. I would load the props on to a truck, known as a chariot, insert a back wheel locker, hook Ben up and then ride down to the face.

Ben was a grey pony and very steady. If the truck came off the rails, he would immediately stop. He would sniff at my jacket if I left it hanging up to see if I had brought him some bread and jam.

Later, I was transferred to another pony driving job which had me supplying two miners with tubs in a development heading. My new pony, Bud and I then took the full tubs to the top of a one-in-three drift, a journey of some three hundred yards. Bud was a clever, little pony and he was fast.

There was another heading which ran parallel to the one in which I worked. They were separated by two ventilation doors which were kept shut.

On one particular day, I popped round to the other heading to see my pal, Bill Butler but I forgot to shut the ventilation doors. When I returned to my own heading, there was no sign of Bud. I looked everywhere but couldn't find him so I decided to go down the return airway as fast as I could. This led to the stables. I looked in Bud's stall which remained empty. I decided to look in the other stalls and there he was, eating another pony's food.

Another of my friends, Jim, who worked at the bottom of the drift, had the biggest pony in the mine. His name was Jack and he pulled eight tubs from the drift bottom to the main haulage way.

If Jim added an extra tub to make it nine in all, Jack would refuse to move and he would back-kick with his hind legs to unhook the tail chain from the front tub. Later, I moved to the Stafford Coal and Iron Company and found myself using a shovel instead of driving a pony.

Finally, I ran my own explosives company and was commissioned to demolish many colliery buildings throughout the United Kingdom.

ROY, BRISK AND FRIENDS

Squadron Leader R.C. Nesbitt
Ex-miner

Between the ages of fifteen and seventeen, I worked in the mine at Boumersund Colliery, Stakeford, Northumberland. During that time, I worked with a number of boys, including Bevin Boys. For a large part of my time as a "Pit boy", I was classified as a driver. My task was to convey the coal tubs to and from the miners at the face or the putters who took on the difficult job of going to the face when things got tough. My ponies were a variety of Dartmoor, Exmoor and the odd Shetland. Their heights ranged from seven to twelve hands. The smallest, Roy, was about thirty years old no more than eight hands. He was mild, easy to handle and quite a delight to work with. On the other hand, Brisk was in his prime, about twelve hands or more and very hard to handle. He bit and kicked and I swear he knew all the tricks in the book. It required four boys to harness him and they dreaded being instructed by the keeper to work with Brisk. On breaking free, he would chase us along the seam until we found a hiding-place and all this in pitch darkness.

With Roy, Smart, Sep or Stamp, I worked what was called the

"X Cut" seam. It was four feet high and at times, we stood in one foot of water. Occasionally, only Roy could be used owing to the limited height. With Brisk, Wavell or Monty, I worked the High Main seam. This was a seam with working heights in excess of six feet. As the only small pony, Roy often worked sixteen hours a day. On one occasion, we boys refused to work him for twenty-four hours, risking stoppage of pay or a dip in the horse trough.

When I was fifteen years of age, my shift was from 5.30a.m. until 2.00p.m. On reaching sixteen, the early shift was from 1.30a.m. until 10.00a.m. Before going on shift, apples were scrumped for the ponies and fed to them during work-time, out of the horse-keeper's view that is. Most ponies could be ridden by lying flat on their backs and travelling into the work- place until it became too low or in sight of the foreman. Only Brisk would not allow us to ride on him. The distance from the stable to the work-place was about one mile and naturally, we looked forward to having a pony that we could ride. Sep would not allow anyone to mount him. Being a clever teenager, I decided one day to try my luck which soon ran out. He threw me off and with a split, bleeding head, I walked one mile in the inky blackness to the shaft. I had lost my lamp. That day, I learned my lesson.

Miners all have mates known in Northumberland as "marras, a Norse word meaning "friend". Most of the ponies I worked with were my friends and the marras of the other boys. They were good company, responsive and at times, loving. On the other hand, most had a spirit and a temperament all their own and would often show it. Regrettably, there were a few putters who occasionally beat their ponies because of stress and fear. Often, the pressure was on to get the coal out and to earn more pay when on piece-work. Then of course, there would be some bad - tempered man who, could not cope with his situation. I say this because it should not go unreported. There were some who were cruel to their ponies and at times, a constant threat to the rest of us who would not put up with it. Having said that, I repeat that most of us loved our ponies and treated them as pets. A pit pony would get you back to the stables in the dark. You just held on to its tail or mane and kept walking. On one occasion, while riding Smart, he would not go on. I dismounted, walked about twenty yards or so, only to find a fall of rock across the path and rails. For direction when working, the ponies always followed the direction of your lamp glow. We sat between the pony's rear end and the front of the tubs we were handling but you had to be ready to jump off when he lifted his tail.

One of the worst journeys I had was when with Roy, I drove about half a mile over steel plates with an injured foreman in the back of the tub. He had been injured by a rock - fall and had a broken shoulder. He lay huddled up in the tub and sobbed with every bump but old Roy had done his good deed for the day.

As a child living in a mining village where the ponies were trained prior to going underground, helping the keepers with the task was commonplace.

Holding the rope while the ponies ran around the ring and helping to put on the 'gears' was fun. This privilege was only granted if you helped clean out the stables. With semi-wild ponies, caution was the order of the day. Today, a youngster would not be allowed to enter a stable housing ponies straight in from the moors. It would be far too dangerous.

On our way to work, we crossed a field that held many ponies. Some were wild and some had finished their stints in the mine because of old age or sickness. I recall vividly one night during the blackout, crossing the field and accidentally kicking something soft and pliable. There was a loud scream, the like of which struck fear into my very soul. Being a fifteen year old, I took off and ran as if the devil himself was after me and I didn't stop running until I reached the pit-head. I had stumbled into a pony lying asleep in the field. At the time the noise was enough to awaken the dead.

I recall many instances while working with the pit ponies. They were our chums, work-mates and pets while working in conditions that would not be accepted in today's society.

Having been a serviceman for thirty-five years and having worked for the military for NATO for fourteen years, I say without hesitation that to work in the coal mines during the war years was every bit more tedious, tiring and dangerous as it was for the majority of military personnel. To sum up, when asked by an off-spring, "What did you do in the war, Daddy?", the answer was so simple: "I worked my butt off in the dark with ponies for pets."

PONY PICTURES

Bill Hudson
Shotton Colliery, Co. Durham

I started work at Shotton Colliery when I was fourteen years of age and spent much of my time there working with pit ponies. I was also a keen photographer and took many pictures of miners and ponies.

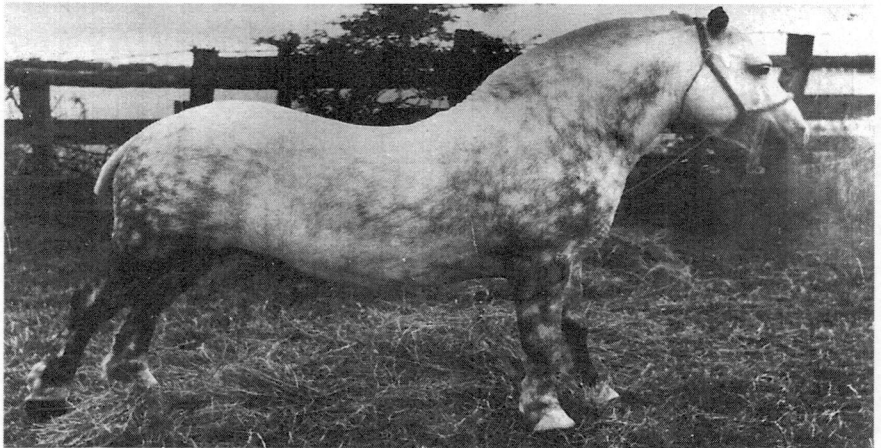

SHOTTON COLLIERY PIT PONY COMPETITION WINNER 1937

TRAINEE MINERS 1932

FOURTEEN-YEAR-OLD PONY DRIVER

TIMBER LEADERS

CAN'T WAIT FOR MY CHOPPY (Finely chopped hay)

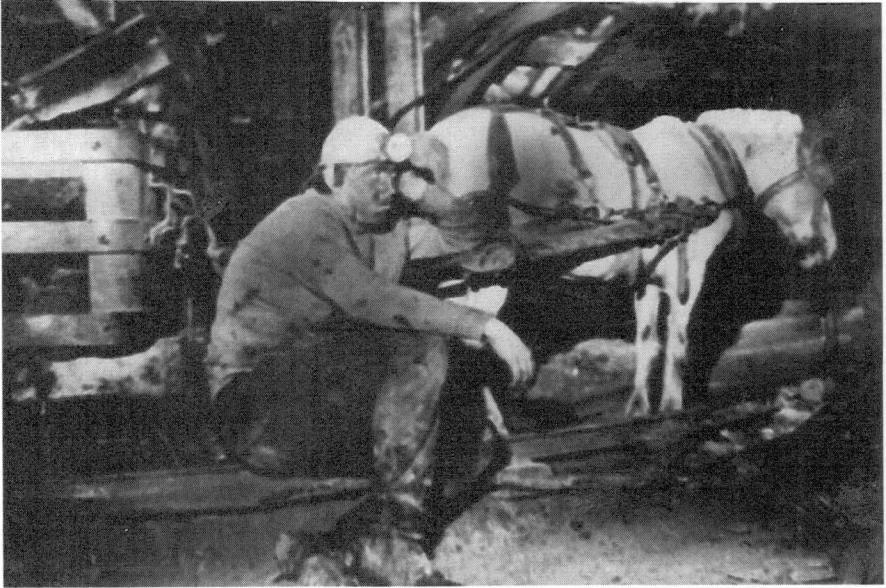

All photographs courtesy of Bill Hudson

LET'S REST AWHILE

ANOTHER LIFE SAVED

Harry Schofield
Bevin Boy, Lofthouse Colliery, Yorkshire

An older miner and I were working on the night shift delivering the daymen's work materials. My job was to clear the track ahead of my work-mate and the pit pony. As I moved forward, I noticed that the roof was 'bitting', a term that we used to mean the roof was moving and that pieces of splintered rock were falling. The pony became agitated and I shouted to my companion that we needed to exercise caution. The older man ordered me to go down the track but I knew that the pony's behaviour gave warning of worse to come. Suddenly, there was a massive fall of rock behind me. I was completely cut off from the pony and his driver. It was a very frightening experience. Fortunately, I had my cap lamp and I spent the rest of the night sealed off and alone. My two companions on the other side of the fall were untouched and had the benefit of an escape route. My plight was duly reported and the next morning, some day shift men dug me out. Had I been killed, it would not have been the pony's fault for he had given us adequate warning of what was to come.

A year later, on my way home after finishing my shift, I was crossing a railway track to catch my train when one of my clogs got caught in the groove of the track. The Sheffield Express came steaming along and I was unable to free myself. Indeed, there was no time to do so and I was hit by the train. The injuries I sustained were far worse than the one I received underground when I lost part of my finger whilst coupling the tubs. I was in hospital for six months and even when discharged, was taken home on a stretcher.

A GIFT FROM HEAVEN

A lower species, so some are told
Nonsense, 'tis a misconception sold
By those proclaiming higher order.
Pray enter our world. Cross the border.

Mice will run and men will shake
As Mother Earth begins to quake.
In accord with nature, we hear and warn
Through a gift bestowed when we were born.

A pony stops full in his tracks
And does not respond to putter's smacks,
For the very air is fraught with dread.
Then a fall seals off the way ahead.

Down the years, men's lives were saved
By an instinct many mortals craved,
With favours returned in countless ways
When perils beset us in that maze.

We know the day, we know the hour,
Attuned to Creation's awesome power.
We entered your world from realms above
And ask for naught but lasting love.

D. Hollows

ENOUGH IS ENOUGH

For the third time, the tub came off the rails.

"Come on, lad," cried the trainer to the Bevin Boy. "Put thy back into it."

To no avail, the exhausted youngster tried to obey the order.

"'ere, you show im 'ow," said the trainer.

Without hesitation, the pony backed up to the tub, bent his forelegs and with the greatest of ease, lifted it back on to the track.

"There, done, see," said the trainer. "Rate tha's goin', tha'll ne'er make a driver."

The pony took off his harness and trotted off down the haulage road.

"'ere, weer does think tha's goin'?" the trainer asked.

"If tha thinks I'm goin' t'do 'is job an' all, tha can think again," came the reply. "I'm off to t'stables for me snap."

A horse or pit pony's daily consumption of food varied according to its size and the work it had to perform but generally, averaged between 20 and 30lbs of provender and hay.

A mixture of oats, Indian corn, bran and peas was a popular meal and well received by the animals.

D. Hollows

PETER AND UBITY

T. Adair
Heworth Colliery

As a young lad working at the belt end, I looked after a pony called Peter. He pulled the chummings up the landing at the belt end and where the coal dropped into the tubs. Peter loved to eat jam butties and I worked with him until I trained for putting. Then I had a pony called Ubity who pulled one tub at a time. Ubity liked any sort of food and wasn't at all fussy. Both ponies were my best mates and I always carried treats for them. I loved them both and I often think of them.

NO PROBLEM

Barbara Wood
Ex-miner's daughter

My father, Thomas Watson, worked down the pit. I do not know if he was ever an expert where horses were concerned but the following incident makes one wonder.

One day, my father came across two men who were having a very difficult time as they tried to get a pony out of the shafts. To no avail, they pushed and pulled and were becoming exasperated. My Dad reached into his pocket and drew out a toffee which he offered to the pony who immediately trotted out of the shafts. I believe that he regularly gave sweets to the ponies which earned him the nickname "Toffee" Watson, a name that didn't greatly appeal to him but which stuck throughout the years.

DOWN TO EXPERIENCE

Geoffrey Binns
Bevin Boy, Woolley Colliery, Barnsley

I worked in the North Thorncliffe seam doing various jobs near the coal-face. The seam was three feet thick at the start, thinning down to two feet over three years. The system worked was called "long wall advance". The coal was undercut to a distance of five feet on the first shift and then the five foot holes were drilled at the top of the seam, fired with explosive on the second shift when it was ready for the colliers on the third shift to shovel the coal on to the conveyor belts running behind them to a central conveying system.

At each end of the coal-face was a place called the "stable hole" where safety-lamps were hung to indicate the level, if any, of methane gas in the air stream and the coal-cutting machines could be turned round. It was up these timber/tail gates leading to the stable holes that pit props were taken in tubs pulled by pit ponies. The tubs containing the pit props were brought into the area by the main haulage system. The ponies were walked by their Bevin Boy drivers from the pit bottom stables down the return airway, a tunnel with nothing in it but warm air to the working area through a variety of airlock doors.

These timber gates were low and narrow, supported by semi-circular steel RSJ's. The single track rails on which the tubs ran were surrounded on each side by loose stones which over the years, had fallen from the roof. If the stones should fall on to the track then the tubs were derailed and it was extremely difficult to scramble up the side of the tub-train to clear the track, lift on the tub and then scramble to the back again. The pit pony knew it was having a rest when such incidents occurred and some of them knew how to scrape the stones on to the track with their fore-feet in order to rest. It was customary when on this duty, for the driver to take some bread for the pony.

One incident which I will never forget took place when I was taking props along the south timber gate. We had to tell the stable foreman, Mr. Turner, which gate we were to traverse so that he could select a pony of the right height. The gate was three feet high so I was given a three foot high Shetland. We were half-way along this very long, narrow road, miles from anywhere when the pony stopped because its collar was caught in a roof girder. We couldn't go either forward or back. I knew the colliers would soon need the props and would not be able to continue their work without them. What a dilemma confronted me. I pushed and shoved to no avail. I even begged the pony (in the only silly pony language I could think of) to help. Time and again, it tried to get through but every attempt failed.

After what seemed an eternity, a light appeared coming toward us and it turned out to be the angry deputy. I explained the difficulty we were in. Then he looked at the pony and swore in language I dare not repeat. The pony bent its legs and moved on quite freely. It certainly knew that I was a Bevin Boy.

On another occasion, a small group of us gathered in the dark return airway ready to take the long walk back to the stables. I was the only Bevin Boy in the group. We were not allowed to ride on the ponies' backs and periodically, Mr. Turner would hide near the stables with his lamp extinguished. If caught, offenders had one pound deducted from their wages. That day, the other lads climbed on to their ponies' backs, leaving the biggest one for me.

They knew that this particular pony was on its first day back after a long stay on the surface following injury. As soon as I sat on its back, it started bucking and kicking and there was nothing to hold on to. I was scared to death and to this day I don't know how I got off without being injured. The pony then took off and ran back to the stables in total darkness. I followed on foot and had to give Mr. Turner a lame excuse as to why the pony had arrived unaccompanied at the stables.

All the pit ponies at our colliery were in very good health and were well-cared for in well-lit stables. Without exception, they had good eyesight and once a year, they were brought to the surface for the Barnsley Feast Week and for the first few days, they would enjoy running amok in the field.

POKER

Bill Ibinson
Dawdon Colliery, Co. Durham

I spent three years in the Dawdon deep mine pit. I was twenty years of age when I started and I am now seventy-seven. In our mine, there were between eighty and one hundred working ponies. The head horse-keeper, Bill Smart, received them in the surface stables where they were shod and sheared by the farriers and horse-keepers. The ponies were very raw and received training before going underground where again they had further training. A pony was never made to work if it was sick or lame. The only trouble was that if there was a shortage in their number, the fit ponies would have to work double shifts.

Putting ponies usually rested from Friday night until early on Monday morning unless, of course, there happened to be a particularly heavy demand for coal. The pony transported all the coal from the face and would haul between twenty to one hundred tubs in a five hours' shift. Where the fuel was easy to extract, they never stopped except to take a drink from the dust-coated water cistern.

In the 1950's during the annual holidays, they were never sent to the surface to enjoy the sunshine and to romp in green fields. Instead, they awaited the return of their putters. Fortunately, the stables were well-lit and they were not neglected.

The pony's haulage apparatus was called 'limbers'. He backed into them and they were fastened to his saddle. The collar chains were known as 'pullings', his saddle chains, 'backings' and his end chains, 'trappings'. As a putter, you sat on the limbers to guide the tubs around bends in the track but it was the little pony who did all the hard work.

One of my ponies had only one eye and was called Poker. They never saw the light of day until they were way past their best and then they were brought to the surface and allowed to run loose in a field near the pit-head.

In the underground stables, sawdust was used, never straw. I assume that the latter presented a flammable threat. The only company the ponies had except for the horse-keeper were the rats. There were far more of them than ponies.

I feel that they were never really appreciated by some in the mining communities although the pony putter and driver did so as they made his job that much easier or harder, whichever the case might be. Piecework was the order of the day and wages depended on output.

Usually, a putter would hang his oil-lamp from his neck which meant that there was very little light but you could depend on those heroic animals who knew every inch of the way, in spite of the dark.

I could write for ever more about the hard work done by our animal friends and I often think of them and their restricted lives.

To be a pit pony meant only one thing: a life of hardship and misery.

There, I rest my case.

A SAD STORY

John Etty
Prince of Wales, Pontefract and Shaw Cross, Dewsbury Collieries

In 1945, I completed my Bevin Boy training at the Prince of Wales Colliery and it was Eddie Waring, well-known television and sports writer who arranged a transfer for me to Shaw Cross. There, I worked with two ponies. They were stabled underground all year except for a two weeks' holiday break in summer when they were taken to the surface. They loved to run about in a field, eat the grass and breathe in the fresh air.

Sadly, one pony was killed when placed in the cage, in a different shaft from mine. He was being taken to the "Black Bed" section, became terrified, kicked through the gate and fell down the shaft. The other ponies were quiet and well-behaved. They never refused to work and were sure-footed over the tram lines. At the end of the shift, they were fed and watered, brushed down and had a bed of hay but no special lighting.

INVITING TROUBLE

Gerry Wardle
Seaton Burn Colliery

I worked at Seaton Burn Colliery, about six miles north of Newcastle-Upon-Tyne. We were taking a pony in bye to the coal-face but the roof was too low for the pony to continue. One lad started to dig into the ground to give the pony more height. On seeing this, a Bevin Boy asked, "Why are you digging the ground? It's the roof his head is touching." Talk about inviting fate.

HARD LABOUR

Jack Thompson
Morrison, Louisa and Eden Collieries (1943-1966)

I had twenty-three years' experience as a miner, working mainly at the coal-face without any training in those days. Having worked for about three years with ponies, you can call that training at the face to become a hewer. We hauled the full tubs filled by the hewer from the face to a flat where empty tubs were stored. The smaller pony was used. It was a single track into the coal-face, only the width and height of a tub. I have known ponies refuse to pull the tubs when in those narrow confines and they would only move when they saw a light from someone approaching them. There were many times when holes had to be dug between the sleepers that held the rails in place to allow the pony to travel, his braffin worn and scrubbed away. These tubs when derailed had to be lifted on with sheer brute strength. The taller pony was used to haul the tubs, usually in two's, three's or even four's from the flat to a much bigger landing from where they were transported by endless rope to the shaft bottom. Some pony drivers would say, "If he can pull three or four, try an extra one." The tracks from the coal-face to the flat were unreliable as they were hurriedly laid and prevented no more than the hauling of two tubs which when made of wood, could hold nine to ten hundredweights each. If made of steel, they were much heavier.

I saw some ponies that were lame and unable to work forced to do a double shift comprising eleven or twelve hours of extremely hard work.

THE PIT PONY

He had served his Lord and master,
Hauled coal from the bowels of the earth,
Lived most of his life in darkness:
For weight in gold was his worth.

No sympathy or help was given
When the pony's end was near.
The pit would have claimed another
And no one would have shed a tear.

Jack Thompson

Sketch courtesy L. Bell, Jack's grandaughter

PONY AND DRIVER

THE PONY PUTTER

Putters and ponies in procession
Along the waggonway:
Tokens jingled on putters' belts
That same road every day.

It seemed so long and tiresome,
Bent double in places low.
Bad light made journeys fearsome
For lads like Bill and Joe.

No lack of courage or indeed, skill,
Hearts as big as they come:
Senses alert were never still
In a body that felt so numb.

Sufferance endured on every day
Took its toll as life moved on:
A price the miner was bound to pay,
Here today, tomorrow gone.

Jack Thompson

In referring to the comradeship that exists between miners he writes, "The miner is a different breed of man, having myself been pulled out from a roof-fall without the rescuers getting the roof supported. Your life was their life. After sixty hours, I regained consciousness and survived, only one of many. I had a fractured skull, leaving it like a corrugated sheet"

A TRIBUTE TO MINERS

The roof caved in without warning,
Crushing my body where I lay.
Senses slipped far into oblivion.
Would I surrender my life this way.

But far from accepting the outcome,
With dangers you're never alone,
My rescuers worked with tenacity
To dig and remove the stone.

Then an arduous trek to the pit-shaft:
Unknown to me how they felt
But miners were used to stumbling.
Their knees were scarred as they knelt.

I have since never met their equal.
Their loyalty shines all around.
No man, they say, is an island:
I experienced that underground.

Jack Thompson

Jack was severely injured in a roof-fall and acknowledges the heroism of his rescuers in this verse.

SPOT - A TRAGIC TALE

Stan Holmes
Cresswell Colliery

I am now approaching my ninetieth year and when I was fourteen, I worked on a farm for six months.

One day, my father said, "I have fixed you up with a job in the pit and you'll be working with the ponies." When I went underground, I was put in charge of a lovely pony called Spot.

I then volunteered for service in the Royal Air Force but after six months I transferred back to the mine under the Bevin Scheme.

Once a year, the ponies were brought to the surface and released into a field. All the locals would gather to watch them and to offer them tit-bits and it was wonderful to see those animals running free. When they saw the daylight after so many months in the darkness of the mine, there was no stopping them. In their new-found freedom, they went wild.

My pony, Spot, was beautiful and we were very close. On one occasion, he appeared at the Royal Windsor Pony Show. When he was twenty-eight years of age and after a virtual life-time underground, I was told to take Spot to the head horse-keeper.

At the time, I wondered why and was so shocked and upset when he said, "Spot is past his prime and worn out. I am afraid I have been ordered to put him down." I couldn't believe it. Then the keeper added, "Spot knows you well and trusts you. I would like you to hold him until the job is done." I flatly refused to comply and another miner took over. After all these years, I have wonderful memories of that loyal, little friend I once knew who is now at peace.

PIT PONY - LITTLE TICK

With putter and miners, December 1913, Yorkshire Coalfield.

FRESH IN MEMORY

Andy Wallace
Bates Colliery, 1959-1986

Nearly fifty years have passed since I worked with the pit ponies. Looking back, some of the things we did with them were just plain crazy, especially when we used to ride them out bye. When we reached the main road where the stables were situated, we really went, I can tell you. The ponies knew they were going back to their warm stables and a meal and were raring to go. The roadway was high and wide and you can picture six or seven young lads racing to the stables. Anyone walking out would keep well clear. The odd deputy would try to stop us but it was of no avail. It was absolutely breath-taking. One particular day, I was following a lad out when his pony stumbled and went down. Such incidents were very rare as they were sure-footed animals. I could not believe it when my pony jumped right over him. Had it been a low tunnel, I might well have broken my back. I halted my pony and went back to see if my marra was injured but both he and the pony were all right and none the worse after the mishap. So off we went on our way again. He was indeed a lucky lad.

Sometimes, we even raced alongside coal-sets going outbye and the loco. Drivers would shake their heads in disbelief but they appreciated that we were young and fool-hardy. We used to earn seven and sixpence wet money and to ensure that we got it, the overman made us carry powder caddies which we had to deliver to his cabin.

Even after all these years, I still remember the names of all the Galloways with whom I worked. There were Boots, Dane, Damper, Captain, HaiA, Hai6B, Maxi, Navy, Lawyer, Bruce, Peter, Pete, Jock, Rob, Tom, Tonto, Royal, Tweed who was killed when hit by a locomotive, Bender, Punch, Victor, Terry, Pat, Wallace, Nailer, Holly and Fox who was also killed.

One day, I was timber leading with Pat who was getting on in years. I actually worked the last shift with him. When I led him to the stables, Ned, the horse-keeper, told me to leave his bridle on, hose him down, take him to the shaft bottom and inform the onsetter that he was there. I knew in my heart what was going to happen. Although Ned had not said so I knew that he was going to be put down. I was very, very upset and as I walked away, Pat whinnied and looked at me as if to say, "Don't leave me."

I had shared my bait with him and my mother always made it a regular practice to put tit-bits in my tin for him. I thought the world of him. He had a heart like a lion and gave his utmost right until the end. The following day, I was given a new pony which had come from a mine that was run down and due for closure. Holly was small, coloured brown and white and stocky. I was dubious at first but he turned out to be an excellent worker and easy to get on with. Together, we carried props to the coal-filling flat which eventually closed and I was transferred to other work. I must add that I still have one of Pat's shoes which is one of my most treasured possessions.

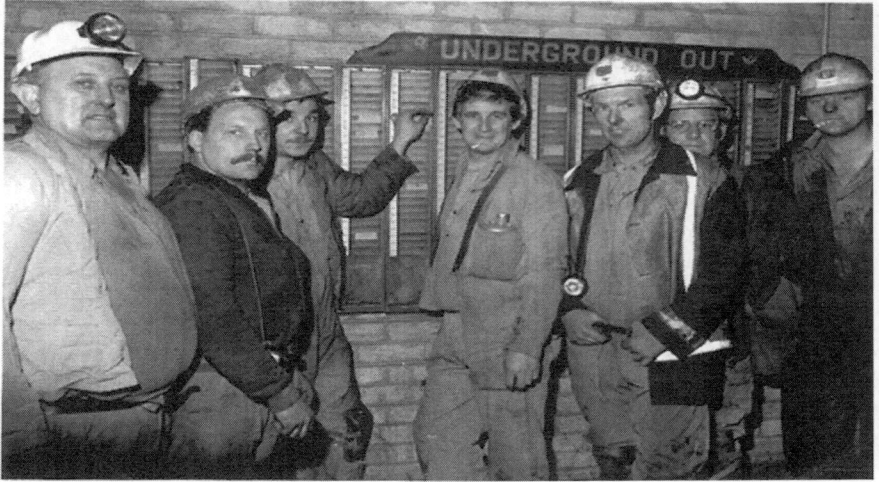

THE LAST SHIFT

Clocking off at Bates Colliery before closure (Andy Wallace third right)

ALAN HAMM LEADS OUT THE PONY, GYPSY

FIDELIS

It is an acknowledged fact that animals accustomed to being in contact with humans can fret and pine when for various reasons they are parted from their owners. The degree of their reactions can depend on the duration of that absence. Their moods may change. They may become morbidly agitated, disinterested in their immediate surroundings, refuse to eat with rapid deterioration of their physical condition and in extreme cases, die.

Many drivers who worked with animals were teenagers and they carried on in that capacity until by virtue of age, they were transferred to other duties. During a pony's lifetime, he might serve with numerous drivers and would develop varying degrees of friendship according to the treatment he received. He could be fastidious over his choice of friends but once established, that bond would be unbreakable. So many records indicate that upon recognising the voice of his carer approaching the stall, there would be an audible surge of activity by the pony, often revealed by the scraping of hooves and a series of excited whinnies.

For the pit pony, encompassed by perpetual darkness who

realises that his friend is no longer present there must be emotional turmoil. Day after day, close interaction with his driver has been sustained and strengthened.

Imagine then what might ensue were the animal's devoted companion to be caught up in tragic circumstances and to lose his life. From time to time, such incidents did happen. That deep and ongoing friendship is suddenly and perforce denied him. There isn't any denying the fact that as with humans the pony will grieve and mourn the loss of a loved one.

A PIT PONY'S FAREWELL

Long ago I had a true friend
And prayed our bond would never end.
I yearned to hear his kindly voice
Which made my very soul rejoice.

With gentle stroke and oft-times praised,
'Twas balm to the dread the darkness raised,
In caverns carved beneath the ground,
Tainted by dust and deafening sound.

One day, my angel did not appear
And I was gripped by doubt and fear:
In vain awaiting that happy call,
Cruelly stilled by a sudden fall.

Sadness blemished my aching heart
For he was gone. We were apart.
I found it hard to bid "Goodbye"
To him ascended to the sky.

Now I am old: my work is done.
Soon, I shall meet that special one.
Together, unfettered we shall both be free
For I loved him and he loved me.

D. Hollows

SNOWBALL AND BOUNCER

Eddie Brown
Bevin Boy, Eastwood Colliery, Nottingham

I worked as a pony driver for seven months and was then transferred to the coal face. I will never forget the time that I spent with my ponies, Snowball and Bouncer. My job was to take the full tubs to the engine-house where they were clipped on to the endless steel cable that ran back to the pit bottom. A one hundred and fifty yards tunnel, some five feet in height was where my pony and I waited to receive the tubs. Snowball, a beautiful brown and white Shetland, was only four feet tall. The face men would hook him on to the full tubs and he would work his way back to me to take off the chain and I would then harness him to the empty tubs and send him back again to the colliers. Bouncer then took over. He was a quick learner and in no time, would take off on his own. When I arrived at the stopping point, he had already turned around, waiting for me to hook him up to the empty tubs. I shared my snap with him and I gave him an apple every day. In the end, he would nudge me with his muzzle which was his way of reminding me that he wanted his favourite tit-bit, an apple, of course.

A pit deputy who saw me clearing a fall of rock with a shovel, approached me and announced that I had used the tool efficiently and it was then that I was moved on to the face. The colliers accepted me as one of them and I spent the rest of my service days working with them. But I must say that I missed my ponies and even today, often think of them.

SIMPSON AND WIMPY

Elizabeth Heskett
Ex-miner's daughter

My Dad who is approaching eighty years, worked with pit ponies for a very long time and he loved them. He worked at Seaham Colliery known as "The Nac" in Durham. The bigger ponies worked in the drift as there was more space and they pulled heavier loads than the small ponies. Simpson, his favourite pony, often shared my father's "bait" of strawberry jam sandwiches and would repeatedly nudge my Dad to get his portion. At the end of the shift, they were led back to the manger in the stables where they were given their "choppy" (hay). Water troughs were filled with cold water enabling them to quench their thirst. There was one really naughty pony called Wimpy who often gave many men a backward kick. One had to learn to read his moods but most of the miners simply refused to work with him. Another pony ate coal dust and couldn't be stopped from doing so. It appears to have been a habit that he developed. My father said that they had a very hard life and often when they were retired, they went to farms and believes that the National Coal Board paid the farmers to look after them for the rest of their lives. Dad suffers from the effects of inhaling coal dust over the years. He has very fond memories of those faithful ponies but adds that neither man nor pony can escape the legacy of the pit.

Elizabeth is the daughter of ex-miner, Joseph Corkhill who loved his ponies and often spoke of them during his long illness. Sadly, Joseph passed away recently and we offer our deepest condolences to his family.

A DISTRESSING EVENT

Ex-putter
Northern Coalfield

A harrowing tale from long ago speaks of a tragedy involving a pony and a child. Once, there was a pony who was extremely handsome. He had a sleek coat and a proud demeanour. For some months, he worked underground with his putter and carried out his duties to the full. One day, he was startled by a sudden loud noise. This unnerved him and he became very agitated, raising his forelegs up and down in quick succession.
It was decided that he should no longer work in the mine. After some discussion regarding his future, a decision was reached. A mine official who had for long admired this beautiful animal, said that it would make a wonderful gift for his young daughter. He lived near to the colliery and owned a field next to his home. Often, the child could be seen by passing miners riding the pony and it was obvious that they had developed a close rapport. One day, the young rider decided to travel along a quiet lane which ran next to the field. All went well until they arrived at a crossroads. There was very little traffic in those days but at the very moment they arrived at the junction, a car roared by. The

frightened pony reared up, throwing the little girl from the saddle. Then, losing its balance, it fell on to its rider crushing her to death. It was a terrible tragedy and cast a gloom over the area. The pony was returned to the field. During the ensuing weeks, it could be seen standing alone and desolate as if overcome by deep sorrow. Its once proud bearing was now gone and miners noticed that it was looking thinner and out of condition. They saw too, that its hooves were in a very sorry state. The local farrier offered to tend the pony but when the men returned to the field to collect it, it had gone and in spite of their making inquiries as to its whereabouts and receiving vague answers, it was never seen again.

THE MAGNIFICENT 'ELEVEN'

Brian Welsh
Hazelrigg and Brenkley Drift Collieries

I was born in a little village called Coxlodge, three miles from Newcastle-upon-Tyne. My first recollections of pit ponies go back to 1950 when my father took me to a field about a mile from our house. There were about twenty-five ponies in the field. They had come straight off the moors and were very wild. They were to become pit ponies. They were broken in at Hazelrigg Pit, three miles or so from our village and were later sent to three or four mines in the area.

When I started work in April 1954, I was a powder-monkey, carrying the caddies of explosives to the pit-head for the piece-workers to collect. I was in charge of a pony which was only three parts broken- in so I had to be very gentle with it. We pulled a rubber sledge onto which the caddies were placed. One had to make sure that the fastening chains were correctly placed so that when the pony stopped pulling, the sledge also stopped dead and did not hit the pony in the hocks. Sometimes, if a pony was hurt or needed stitches to an injury, he would be taken up to the bank and treated in the stables. Then he would work with one of the boys in the screens for two weeks. Their job was to carry props in the timber-yard. After that, the pony was sent back down the pit. The first pony I had was called Toff. He was big, soft and a delight to work with. As soon as he heard my voice as I entered the stables, he would whinny until I reached his stall. One day, I was asked by the horse-keeper to take on another pony to accompany Toff. His name was Piper, the biggest pony in the pit. For working with two horses, I was paid one shilling per week extra. After two weeks of working with them, it was like a sing-song when I entered the stables and they whinnied in unison at the sound of my voice. One night, the stables were very quiet. Toff and Piper had been sent to another pit three miles away. They were to be used by salvage men because of their size and strength. I was then given a pony called Duke who was tall but more like a racehorse than a pit pony. He was all right and we worked well together. My extra shilling a week was withheld until I was asked to take on a new pony named Pop. He was a beautiful Skewbald. When I was seventeen, it was my turn to go pony-putting, pulling out coal tubs with a pony from a district called Board and Wall . There was no conveyor-belt, only tubs and my ponies were now Kelly and Turpin with whom I worked for two years. Both were first-class ponies. Kelly was very strong and slow and Turpin just the opposite being both light and fast. When the putting flats were stopped, three of my 'marras' and I were sent on salvage work. We were given four of the biggest and strongest ponies in the mine. They were called Colin, Boxer, Lion and Tank. They were very quiet and soon Don was added to the quartet He was a handful but he finally settled down. I worked with Don until I was transferred to face-work and it was a case of no more ponies, just a shovel, pick and axe.

In 1960, most of the ponies went to different pits and as I worked on a long-wall face, I did not see much of them. That is, until we were moved to another mine called Brenkley Drift. Thereafter, we saw a lot of the ponies because there weren't any stables underground and they were all brought up to the bank after each shift Before that, some had never seen daylight in over twenty years.

When the mines closed, some of the ponies were sold off privately but most of the older ones were sent to a holiday park about twenty-five miles away. There, they ran in the fields and enjoyed their new-found freedom until age got the better of them.

I could speak at even greater length about our animal friends. They were indeed the backbone of the coalfields.

UNKNOWN SOURCE

J.N. Farrell

I have had this poem for many years. I do not know who wrote it but perhaps it records the situation that existed in years gone by. I always looked after my pony when putting. Those animals were our mates who helped you earn a living.

THE DEATH OF A PIT PONY

This is a story of Mint, my pony friend
Whose life was drawn to a tragic end,
By some dirty blackguard from the N.C.B.
Who didn't give a damn for my pony or me.

We went down the pit, me and my friend:
We didn't know his life was near its end.
We started his shift: for work he was prepared.
Little did we know in a few hours he would be dead.

He was old and weary and needed a rest
But he kept on going, like one of the best.
Sometimes, he fell down and collapsed on the ground
And it took him a while to get pulled around.

We finished our shift and went outbye.
We still did not know old Mint had to die.
He went to the bank that bright October day
And was shot without a drink or a mouthful of hay

In pastures green, his tiredness would have mended
And given him recompense for services rendered
But this was too expensive, so they told me:
It couldn't be afforded by his owners, the N.C.B.

BANTRY

Beryl Ungate
Widow of Leonard, Bevin Boy, Penallta Colliery

My late husband, Leonard Ungate, originated from Wales but was living in Middlesex when his number came up to serve in the mines. He was sent to Oakdale before transferring to Penallta Colliery where he worked for three years and ten months. An injury to his hand left him with a deformed finger. Working with pit ponies revealed how canny and perceptive they were. One notorious pony was well known for gathering speed on sections of the track which had a kink in the rail. Despite the drover's shouting in Welsh which Len understood, 'Bantry' would have the trams derailed and earn himself a rest. Nuzzling the miners' snap tins would be rewarded with a jam sandwich or the occasional apple. On one particular shift when my husband was working on the coal-face, no amount of pushing and shouting would prompt 'Bantry' to move. Apparently, the roof had moved during the night and props and blocks had split. Suddenly, there was a fall of rock, trapping and burying men at the face. Len was the only Bevin Boy among them. He truly believed that his number was up. Lying in total darkness and covered in coal, listening to the trapped men calling to one another was a horrible experience and I firmly feel that the subsequent nightmares he experienced throughout his life were attributable to that incident. Eventually, the men were rescued, cut and bruised but were expected to report for duty the next day. 'Bantry's obstinacy on that day most certainly saved the lives of many miners. To see those ponies being taken to the surface for their annual break, kicking their legs and rolling in green fields, brought my husband great pleasure and on his passing, a substantial donation was made to the Pit Pony Sanctuary, Pontypridd.

Leonard was a man of the valleys and he understood the way of life in a mining community.

His ashes were scattered in the churchyard of St. Peter's, Cockett, near Swansea, where he was christened and where his family worshipped. I pray that he now rests in peace.

VERITY AND EAGLE

J. Lockhart
Dinnington Main Colliery

I remember one pony in particular when I was at Dinnington Main Colliery. His name was 'Verity' . I was told that he was hard of hearing and to get him to start working when hauling the tubs, you had to pull his tail once and to stop him, twice. Another one called 'Eagle' broke my arm. He was wild and ran straight into a roof-fall. I sustained my injury trying to control him. I thought this was very unusual behaviour for ponies were known to sense a fall and would not budge until the danger had passed. I later learned that 'Eagle' was in his first year down the mine.

THE TOFF

H. Griffiths
Bevin Boy, Llanbradach Colliery

I always said that the term 'pit pony' was a misnomer. Where I worked, they were big, strong horses who could pull a tram full of coal with two wheels spragged and the haulier on the bar. I was probably the only Bevin Boy who went underground wearing a Savile Row jacket given to me by my friend's mother. At every opportunity, I showed my colleagues the label and was really proud when they looked at me in amazement. Time can soften the memory but mining was a lousy job, as well as being dirty and dangerous and I certainly hadn't any regrets when I was demobbed.

TOO LATE FOR SO MANY

It has recently been claimed by experts that horses can suffer from Seasonal Affective Disorder with accompanying depression, just like humans.

A lady therapist asserts that the remedy lies in subjecting them to a massive dose of daylight. She uses special light boxes which emit a minimum of ten times more light than that of a normal bulb but eliminate harmful UV rays. The system was tested on a dejected horse which had been pronounced dangerous by its owner. After treatment, a great improvement in its behaviour was noted. Many pit ponies spent their whole lives underground, deprived of fresh air, adequate exercise facilities and above all, daylight and never resurfaced until their days were spent.

In view of these latest findings, it is miraculous that those noble animals responded so well to their keepers and performed their arduous duties with dogged determination, dignity and stoicism.

D. Hollows

FOOD FOR THOUGHT

Miners were well aware of the diverse personality traits of the horses and ponies. Some would refuse to co-operate if they felt that they were burdened by additional loads which indicates that they recognised their own physical limitations. One such pony would lie down in the middle of the track until the extra weight was removed. When satisfied, he would rise to his feet and calmly proceed down the haulage-way as if nothing had happened. His display of equine passive resistance was repeated on numerous occasions and he never failed to emerge the victor. It was not unknown for thirsty animals to seek out the miners' water flasks, remove the corks with their teeth and imbibe the refreshing contents. Whilst all the ponies enjoyed the treats of carrots, bread crusts, slices of cake and apples, there were some who relished the additional bonus of chewing tobacco used by the miners to moisten their mouths.

One must assume that they appreciated the salutary effects of this practice. Again, a pinch of snuff was welcomed for they learned that inhaling powdered tobacco to clear their nostrils of accumulated dust was therapeutic. They were intelligent creatures and working so closely with their male counterparts, little would escape their attention. Indeed, they were able to observe the miners' rituals and habits at first hand.

It is recorded that a pony which was jet black in colour was from time to time, averse to working and he would conceal himself near to a manhole. Perfectly camouflaged in the darkness, he would remain still until the miners who were unaware of his presence, had passed by. Thereupon, he would make his way back to the stables for a rest and a snack which more often than not, had been prepared for another animal and without any hesitation, would consume it.

Deep under the surface, lay an alien world where hardship, tragedy and suffering for both the miner and his animal charges were omnipresent. In those adverse conditions, a firm bond of friendship and interdependence was established. There were countless incidents when the ponies provided a counterbalance of unexpected and humorous activity which helped nullify the bleakness of mining's toil. The lives of many miners were saved by the instincts and astuteness of those loyal animals. The Heaven-sent gifts that they displayed are bestowed upon all creatures and often transcend those of man himself. One can only wonder at the marvels of God's creation and leave us to question our own limitations.

D. Hollows

ENSLAVEMENT

The miner's lot has always been demanding and beset by many dangers. Nowadays, one may find it hard to fully appreciate the suffering he once underwent to provide for his family. By 1730, the annual coal output had risen to seven million tons. In those days, life was cheap, the death rate being naturally regulated by disease as well as hard work. Miners were high in the league on both counts and the dangerous surroundings and methods of working did nothing to ease matters. Miners, their wives and children were all employed as a team in coal extraction.

If they were lucky, they were carried up and down the shaft by hanging on to a rope whilst a winch, gin or whimgin did the raising or lowering. The latter two were horizontal drums rotationally propelled by man or horse-power, very similar in operation to an early ship's capstan.

Ladder pits were common and everybody or everything entering or leaving the mine was subjected to the rigours of using rickety wooden ladders. Indeed, the women and children were well-versed in transporting baskets of coal to the surface by this method, often in conditions of almost total darkness and accidents were common. Depths of 61 metres were not unusual for ladder pits. The landowner held the mineral rights at this time and an agent would be appointed to manage the affairs of his mines. Coal was king and a landowner in a coalfield quickly became very wealthy. Not every mine owner was uncaring but his ilk were few and far between. Very often, the miner was obliged to have his tools repaired by the mine's blacksmith. His wife would be encouraged to buy the family groceries and other items from the mine-owned shop, all goods being at elevated prices that often left the family with little or nothing to support itself.

The very hovel in which they lived was often a 'tied' property and it was a frequent occurrence to see mining families evicted on to the street for some minor misdemeanour, or because the breadwinner was injured, ill or just too old to work.

Below ground, life was even harder. Often, for up to fourteen hours a day, the menfolk would hew the coal and the women and children transport it to the pit bottom and in ladder and adit mines, to the surface. The women would wear a tight-fitting harness to pull the 'corves' (large baskets), which were mounted on sleds, over the uneven tunnel floors. An older child would assist by pushing the heavy burden, often up steep inclines to the shaft bottom. Later, wheeled trucks or tubs were used and life was made a little easier when the tubs were made to run on rails. The easier it became to pull them, the larger and heavier the tubs became. A miner's life was far from ideal. Accidents and explosions were frequent, often, everyday occurrences. Times were hard and lung-related diseases were something to try and forget about until they killed you. There was no Health and Safety legislation and if a miner wouldn't do the job, there was always one behind him who would. Perhaps one of the most pernicious effects on a miner's livelihood was the Sliding Scale. This was a means of regulating pay to the selling price of coal. In times of trade depression and there were plenty of those, the price of coal would fall on the market-place and the miners would have their pay cut accordingly. The local militia swiftly dealt with any unrest and after a few heads had been cracked open, things quickly got back to the normal levels of poverty.

There was no Welfare State to fall back on in those days.

By the first quarter of the nineteenth century, the Government began to look at the conditions relating to coal mining. Usually such scrutiny was as a result of a particularly bad accident. Take for instance, the Hartley Pit in the North-East of England. This colliery, like many others, had only one shaft. Positioned over the shaft was a pumping engine and the attached rods ran down the shaft to the sump. The pumping engine was working all day, every day, to clear the mine of water until January 1862 when the beam broke. The beam end crashed down the shaft, taking all in its path with it and completely destroying the ventilation in the process. The shaft was blocked and the two hundred and four souls down the mine died from asphyxiation before the debris could be cleared. Following this tragedy, legislation was put in place which meant that every deep coal mine had to have two shafts so that an alternative method of entrance and exit was always available.

By 1840, the Government was expressing concern for the welfare of women and children employed underground, more from a moral standpoint than safety implications and it was decided to invoke legislation to prevent such employment. Two august bodies were engaged in reviewing the situation, the South Shields Committee and a Royal Commission (The Children's Employment Commission). The information elicited revealed the existence of a state of affairs far worse than expected. Lord Ashley (afterwards, Lord Shaftesbury) introduced a measure prohibiting the employment of women and girls underground and restricting the employment of boys. The measure received the Royal Assent on the 10th August 1842 and came into full effect on the 1st March 1843. After this date, it became illegal to employ any females underground or any boys under the age of 10 years with the exception of boys who were already employed in the pits at the time. This decision was very unpopular with the miners for they would now have to pay other men to assist them in winning the coal, the miners themselves being self-employed.

For several years after this restriction was introduced, disguise was the order of the day, with the usual blind-eyed philosophy adopted by the mine manager and officials.

Slowly but surely from the mid-nineteenth century, conditions in the mines were drastically improved. This was ably assisted by the formation and appointment of the Mines Inspectorate and improvements in technology, particularly with regard to mine ventilation and methods of working.

Mining was and always will be, a dangerous occupation carried out in an unforgiving environment. Every pit village graveyard bears testimony to that.

Reproduced by kind permission of Geoffrey Jones from his publication entitled 'Coal'.

Geoff is Chairman of the Red Rose Steam Society, Astley Green Colliery Museum, Higher Green Lane, Astley, Tyldesley, Manchester M29 7JB.

Site Opening Times:
Sunday   10.30   to   5.00 p.m.
Tuesday   12.30   to   5.00 p.m.
Thursday 12.30   to   5.00 p.m.
Plus all Bank Holidays except Christmas Day.

Private parties can be catered for all the year round. A slide show can be arranged by prior appointment.

For further information, please contact the Secretary at the address shown.

NEW HARTLEY COLLIERY DISASTER (1862)

As a result of the tragedy, 400 widows and orphans were left. The ages of the victims ranged from 11 years to 70 years.

The manager of the mine was Joseph Humble, the great, great, great grandfather of the well-known TV personality, Kate Humble. Unable to gain access underground, he spent days and nights on the surface doing whatever he could which was limited. It took more than a week to reach the dead miners. Joseph's nephew was listed among the casualties. One can appreciate the feeling of helplessness and the mental suffering that he must have experienced. A good leader always shows concern for the welfare of those who serve him and he was no exception.

Devastated, he left the area and opened up a business in Durham.

Later, it was disclosed that prior to the accident, the mine's owners had been advised to sink a new shaft which would have given the men a chance of survival but that they had refused to do so.

The cost of so doing would have amounted to a mere £200, just less than £1 per man and boy.

MINERS

Why do I admire you,
What do I see there,
Is it the soft smile on your lips
Or the shine on your well-washed hair?

No, it's the something special
You have been destined to do,
The experience I see in your eyes
That draws me to you.

In all of your daily lives,
You have known both Heaven and Hell:
One is the glorious sunlight,
The other, the pit with its strange small.

Shift after long stinking shift,
I know of your mortal danger:
Death, accidents, limbs lost,
To you they are no stranger.

The courage and protective care
Of one miner for another,
It is a feeling known to a few,
As though each is the other's brother.

Every man depends on the next,
To keep each safe and sound.
There is a special unity,
I sense you have underground.

Whenever I go on a journey
On land, sea or by air,
I can pick you out of many
Because of the great man I see there.

Strength, might, grit and guts,
On your face I can see.
The greatest in all the world:
That is what you are to me.

Mary N. Bell
Easington Writers

WAILING AND GNASHING
(Based on a true incident)

Down t'shaft they plunged to start a new day.
"Cheer up, fellers. Gorra joke," shouted Ray.
They listened, they laughed as they shot down deep
But Owd Keith, the driller, began to weep.

"What's matter, Keith? Didna like me tale?"
"It ain't that," he replied and started to wail.
"What is it then? Can't be that bad.
Tha's allus bin such a lively lad."

"I know I 'ave," sobbed grieving Keith.
"Trouble is . I've just lost me teeth."
"Run off, 'ave they?" asked Sammy Page.
"Nay, I recall I 'ad 'em when I stepped in t' cage."

"Weer are they then? I can't see nowt."
"Bottom o' t' shaft, I 'ave no doubt."
"Them teeth's bin trouble sin' day I got 'em.
Wish I'd stayed gummy. I 'ate 'em rotten."

"If tha feels like tha', why ar't so sad?"
"Cos I can't munch me snap. That's why, me lad."
Well if tha's really clemt, tha can suck thy thumb.
Don't mean it, owd lad. Just 'avin' some fun."

"Tha'll be all reet, Keith, 'ave no fear,"
Said Sam. "I've just 'ad a smashin' idea.
Reckon me mouth's about t'same size as thine,
So when I've 'ad me butties, tha can borrer mine."

D. Hollows
Clemed / Clemt: dialect term meaning either 'cold' or 'hungry', depending on context.

GOD-GIVEN GIFTS

Recently, a retired collier referred to the aesthetic qualities inherent in the miner's make-up.

To the uninitiated, little is known about them but as a former Bevin Boy, I was privileged to work with them and to observe at first hand, their latent talents. Their lives were a combination of toil and danger and among them, I found budding authors, poets, artists, singers, musicians, humorists and sportsmen.

Colliery brass-bands reveal a deep love of music and a sense of pride in belonging to a vast brotherhood They embrace the gift of life and seem to be in accord with its rhythm. One becomes well aware of this when one is confined in the bowels of the earth. Thanks to them, there is an abundance of tangible evidence confirming their varied extraneous skills. One can only appreciate and marvel at the depth of sincerity shown.

Steve, one of my underground colleagues, was a budding novelist and lay preacher who when time permitted, jotted down his ideas for plots. George was an accomplished vocalist. During the silence of snap-time, his rich tones could be heard echoing through the galleries, earning the repetitive comment, "'ark, lads, Big George is at it again."

It was a balm and welcome therapy to all within earshot.

Spontaneous humour too, was ongoing and so often helped allay the fears of young men drafted into an alien world.

For me, it is an honour to count among my friends a body of hard-working, loyal and courageous men who would not hesitate to sacrifice their lives to save a comrade. They represent a unique corporate spirit which can be traced back to mining's earliest days and there you have a picture of the typical miner.

D. Hollows

KINDRED SPIRITS (TOM AND TED)

Tom Lamb is a classic example of miner cum artist. His works extend from the depths of the earth to reach those who hitherto were unaware of the heavy demands made upon men in that subterranean world.

When he was young, he contracted diphtheria and during his period of convalescence, discovered that he had an artistic bent and he was destined to become a prolific recorder of miners at work.

The high, white-painted walls at the bottom of the shaft became his canvas upon which and initially using axle-grease, he drew portraits of his colleagues. His manager was so pleased with the result that he instructed the miners to leave them untouched and they now remain undisturbed in the sealed mine.

Tom exhibited his work in many parts of the country, including Hobart House, London and the Tate Gallery.

Upon closure of the Craghead Colliery, Tom became an assistant at the Durham Light Infantry and Art Gallery where he was well-qualified to use his artistic expertise when guiding visitors.

Tom observed in an introduction to one of his exhibitions entitled 'My Mining Days', "People talk about the nostalgic element in my mining paintings but at the time, the scenes set down in my sketchbook were far from nostalgic. They were of a contemporary, cruel, ugly and inescapable life and its physical labour.

When I went to work at the Busty Pit, my inspiration came from apprehension and foreboding. Here was to be an unforgettable experience. Essentially, it was drawing for its own sake. I became fascinated, so drawing from life was an important part of my early training"

I must also speak of my close friend, Ted Holloway. As artists and miners, it was the most monumental experience for both of us to portray our fellow miners as they toiled with strained, tensed muscles in the dignity of physical labour in the dark, wet and dangerous conditions underground.

The figures struck a deep chord and we were very aware of an emotional and visual experience brought about by seeing the courage, sorrow and sometimes, even death of the working miner in his environment. We hope that the drawings and paintings reflect the' fullness of the dramatic narrative of the miner's life underground."

Recently, there was an exhibition of Tom's art work at the National Mining Museum, Caphouse Colliery, Wakefield and it was dedicated to his brother, Jacky, who frequently modelled for him.

An example of Tom's work at the shaft bottom, using the medium of axle grease.

Jacky Gannin To The Pit

On a winters morning in the 1950s a man with his trousers
tucked into his turned down Wellington boot tops, his rough
overcoat buttoned up against the freezing wind and snow,
climbed the steep road that leads from Peartree to
Craghead Colliery standing on the heights.
As he turned the corner he felt the full force of the winter
wind.
His thoughts were of his wife and children safely snuggled
up in bed in their warm, comfortable home.
After a long day of killing work in the mine he would walk
the two miles home again.

To me he was a great man, he was my brother.

© Tom Lamb.

Reproduced by kind permission of Tom Lamb

RAW SAUSAGES FOR HIS BAIT

This was a very laughable incident as we unwrapped our baits.
We couldn't believe our eyes when Tommy Randle, with a look of utter bewilderment, held up raw sausages. At that time in the 1940's, everything was wrapped up in newspaper. As was the norm, the wife would put up her husband's bait and on that day, Mrs. Randle had come home from the butcher's with the sausages wrapped in newspaper.
So, Tommy, leaving for work, mistakenly picked up the sausages, not his bait. After the laughter, we shared our bait with him.

Photograph by John Hughes, Colliery Manager

Using chalk and grease on a piece of conveyor sheeting, Tom displays his drawing of a miner testing his safety-lamp. The picture was hung in the lamp-room as a constant reminder to the men to test their lamps before going underground.

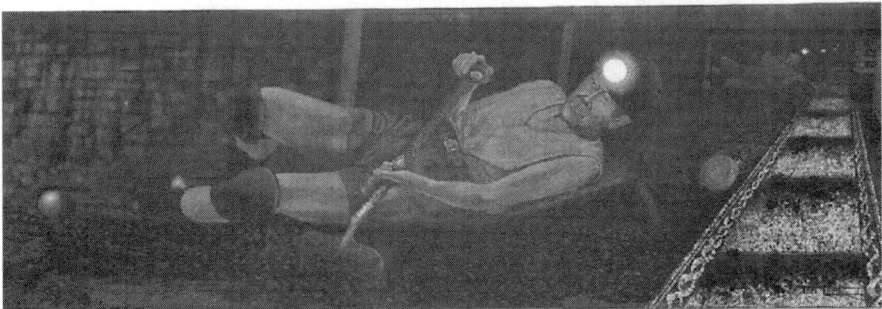

FILLER IN A 24" SEAM

Drawings courtesy of Tom Lamb

HEWER AND PUTTER IN THE BUSTY PIT

From a painting by Tom Lamb, ex-miner and artist

EPITAPH FOR A PIT PONY

THE BAIT SNATCHER

Tom Lamb
Ex-miner, Thomas Pit, Craghead and Busty Seam

It was 1944-1945 when young pit lads walking to Craghead Colliery from the outlying villages (Blackhouse, Burnhope and Grange Villa), fell prey to a tramp and had their bait taken from them.

There was no transport in those days. The lads were advised to walk to the pit in groups, if possible. But as for me, I had been transferred from the screens to the pit head baths and the shift times were different from those of the other lads. I had to walk the four miles from Blackhouse to Craghead along a very dark country lane. To be alone at 2.00 a.m. at the age of fifteen, walking this lane, was a bit scary.

So I fell prey to this tramp and what a terrifying experience it was. A moving figure emerged from the hedge, a shady figure stepping out from a dark background of foliage. He had long hair and a beard and he stood in front of me, a large stick raised high. The silence of the night was broken by his gruff voice shouting, "Give me your bait or I'll whack you one."

Cold and shaking, I was indeed facing the bait snatcher. I looked around hopelessly for some means of escape but there was only one answer to this desperate state of affairs: I had to give up my bait.

After that, I took two baits with me, one for the tramp and one for me. We put a crumpled laxative in his.

It all came to a sudden end when, at Grange Villa, men ganged up on him, took most of his clothes off and tarred and feathered him.

Looking back now, it must have been very funny to see that tramp getting his just desserts.

The whole episode was a mixture of tragedy and comedy.

Bait – lunch

Reproduced by kind permission of Tom Lamb

THE BAIT SNATCHER

IN MITIGATION

Tom aptly describes the incident involving the bait snatcher as a "mixture of tragedy and comedy". This was by no means, a single event for there were numerous repetitions of this type of misdeed reported in various areas. Indeed, unacceptable behaviour merits some form of censure but one feels it necessary to question and to identify the motives for such acts.

In the period between the two World Wars, many industrial workers in the North lost their jobs. Miners, shipbuilders, cotton and woollen weavers were badly affected. Money was at a premium. An overwhelming burden now rested on the shoulders of those unfortunates. Hunger was endemic and illness was rife. Children suffered from rickets due to vitamin deficiency and to counteract this, school milk was introduced. Often, the young would be sent to their beds at lunch-time for on their meagre diets, it was considered unwise for them to expend too much energy. Saving grace came in the presence of the pawn- broker. Overnight, their numbers grew and they did well out of the depression. Derelict properties were converted into shops who advertised their role by displaying three brass balls on the outer wall of the building. Goods could be exchanged for cash which helped feed the family and later, could be redeemed by tendering ones personal pawn ticket and an agreed sum of money to the pawnbroker.

As a child, I recall hearing my parents and grandparents discussing the Jarrow March that had taken place some years previously when men walked several hundred miles to seek better pay and conditions. My father, a teenage survivor of the Gallipoli campaign, held strong views on the injustices meted out to so many who, less than a decade before, had sacrificed so much. Being far too young to have witnessed the march, I was proud to learn that my family had raised funds and donated food in support of those involved.

I remember that during the 1930's, I saw numerous down at heel characters wandering the streets and inviting recompense from passers-by. Many of them slept outdoors and were obviously homeless, existing solely on the hand-outs of well-wishers. I could not help but notice that they had one thing in common. Their lack-lustre eyes and their gaunt, haunted faces made one feel that they dwelt in a world detached from reality. It seemed as if they had surrendered all hope of redeeming themselves and were now resigned to lives of uncertainty, deprivation and abject poverty.

Yet there was light in that darkness for there were others who made every effort to re-establish themselves into society and rightfully claim their place. Some travelled from house to house, offering to do odd jobs or to stain and laboriously paint front doors so that they appeared to have been regrained. There was a regular visitor to our street who stooped under the weight of assorted musical instruments, including a large drum to which were attached two cymbals. This one-man band was a popular attraction for the local children who were eager to fill his cap with coppers.

But most moving of all was the lonely figure who, on a weekly basis, went from door to door. He was blind and he carried a tray filled with buttons, cottons, needles and ribbons. On his left breast, he had a row of medals as had the musician and so many of the homeless I had seen. I then realised that these were men who had survived the horrors of the Great War. Their lives had been stained by their experiences and while there were those who were learning to pick up the threads of normal living again, others seemed to have given up all hope.

It is not unreasonable to assume that our bait snatchers were part of that latter group. They too, may well have been the debris of a bitter conflict that had claimed the lives of so many and as I recount my tale, I can only feel a great sadness coupled with deep gratitude.

D. Hollows

A LEGACY OF WAR

Long ago, when just a mere lad,
A grey-faced soul made me so sad:
With shuffling gait evoking piteous stares,
Shaking a tin and selling his wares.

He displayed his buttons, needles and threads.
I sensed his world was beset by dreads.
On his threadbare jacket, some medals were sewn
And in stripling eyes, his stature had grown.

His gaze was blank, his features sore lined:
Innocence lost, now frail, now blind.
There shone his record of suffering and pain:
The debris of conflict and hard-won gain.

In trenches deep, in clawing mud
And that Hell forever drenched in blood,
Seeing comrades lost as lives they yield,
Now finding Peace in a foreign field.

I watched him turn and tap his slow way
Into morning mist and another drear day.
The tears that I shed were a silent toast
To that grey-faced man who seemed but a ghost.

D. Hollows

EPITAPH FOR A PIT PONY

Tom Lamb
Ex-miner, Thomas Pit, Craghead and Busty Seam

One morning in the summer of 1945, a timber tram came to the surface from the Thomas Pit, Craghead, with a dead pony inside. The unfortunate pony had been killed in an accident. On the side of the tram was written:

"To shut me from the light of the sky and the sights of the fields and clouds-without these things I cannot live. My favourite pony, Tramp R.I.P. George"

We were all feeling very sad but none more so than George, the Bevin Boy who was conscripted from Somerset to work in the Durham coalfields. He had been a farmer working with shire horses on his uncle's farm.

He was sent to the Thomas Pit, Craghead to look after the pit ponies at the shaft bottom. Tramp was a painful loss to him and in his grief, he wrote those moving words, expressing his feeling of shame that the ponies were shut away in the mines.

Tramp was a Shetland pony about seven hands (28 inches or 71 centimetres) tall at the shoulder. Soon a close bond between Tramp and George began and so it was a personal tragedy weighing him down.

Later that evening, with special consent from the Manager and with two close friends, George buried Tramp in a corner of the field near the pit-head baths.

This tragic incident shocked this unashamed animal lover and it made him very unhappy every time he saw Tramp's stall.

He was therefore transferred for the last six months before his demobilisation from the Thomas Pit to the Busty Seam that had no ponies.

It was now that I was introduced to George when he came to work with me on the rope-ends at the shaft bottom.

George was a gentle man, well-built six feet tall, a man of exceptional literacy and well-educated. He said he would have his own farm one day, I told him that I was deeply moved by the writing on the tram.

He replied, "It was a quotation from Saint Joan, which summed up my feelings for those ponies who came to the surface for only one week each year when the pits are on the annual holidays."

He added, "Tramp stole my heart. I would go to a local farm to get the little fellow some linseed cake and beans which were intended for the sheep. There's nothing like linseed cake for putting a gloss on their coats."

On the last day of George's release from the pit, he was presented with the name sign from Tramp's stall but before he returned home to Somerset, he had one last thing to do.

He went to Tramp's grave and with tears in his eyes, said 'Goodbye' to his little friend for the last time.

'Epitaph for a Pit Pony'" is reproduced by kind permission of the author, Tom Lamb and first appeared in 'Bands and Banners' magazine, No. 6, Summer, 2000.

KINDRED SPIRITS (TED)

Ted Holloway was born in the small village of Upham in Hampshire. He was surrounded by the beauty of the countryside and totally absorbed its atmosphere which bestowed upon him both poetic and artistic capabilities. As a schoolboy, he excelled at arts and crafts and was a budding wood carver.

When he was fifteen, he became a forester and enjoyed working close to nature. Then he was conscripted as a Bevin Boy.

Chance brought Ted and Tom together for they found themselves working in the same mine and as a result of their mutual interest in drawing and painting, they became lifelong friends. As with Tom, Ted too, drew pictures on those subterranean walls and with the closure of the mine, they lie buried there to this day.

Upon demobilisation, Ted returned home but five years later, found himself back at Craghead Colliery. Ted's and Tom's fascination for drawing and painting prompted them to cycle many miles together in order to find suitable settings for their landscapes and their output was prolific.

For ever seeking to improve his skills, Ted studied Art at Durham University and later, at the Sunderland College of Art. Finally, he was awarded a Teaching Diploma at Goldsmith's College, University of London and went on to become a lecturer.

He retired from teaching in 1981 so that he might pursue his interest in full-time painting. From his early days, Ted was an avid reader of myths and legends and many of his later works are based on Celtic stories.

Sadly, he died on a painting trip to Scotland in 1987 but his spirit lives on in the wonderfully talented paintings and wood-carvings that he bequeathed for future generations to enjoy and admire.

It is Ted's legacy to us all which had its beginning amidst the fields, flowers and wild-life of a small Hampshire village so long ago.

Referring to her late husband, Gill Holloway writes, "Ted loved animals and for quite a time in the pit, he had not only his own special pony but he seemed to be in overall charge of the ponies. I well remember as a child in Durham, seeing the ponies coming up from underground and being released into fields full of buttercups. There, they would gallop and buck with joy.

For a long time, I had a lovely, old ex-pit pony called Diana who had a foal which we called Donald. Diana died and I reared her foal on a bottle. He was so very small.

Ted's original mining works are now in a collection of Northern Industrial Art which is being developed for display in Bishop Auckland."

Photograph courtesy John Lamb

Ted with his whippet, Simon in Ireland (1983) and pursuing his interest in Celtic Art.

Courtesy of Mrs. Gill Holloway

MINERS

All artwork courtesy of Mrs. Gill Holloway

TONY HILTON REMEMBERED

Tony Hilton was a talented Cheshire poet who, as with Ted Holloway, had an affinity with nature which was expressed in the many verses that he wrote. He was a happily-married man who liked nothing better than to wander through the rural surroundings of Dunham Massey Hall, Altrincham, observing the wild life and recording his thoughts. His works gave so much pleasure to his many readers and over the years, he raised thousands of pounds for charity.

Tony marvelled at the wonders of creation and had deep feeling for all living things. Sadly, he recently passed away but he has left a wonderful legacy of verse to be enjoyed by others down the years. Referring to his limited life-span and the subjects of his works, an admirer commented, "It is as if he walked hand in hand with God" and the sincerity and love that his writings express only serve to confirm that close proximity.

Among his poems, he wrote a dedication to miners, revealing his ability to sympathise with the plight of those less fortunate whose working lives are fraught with danger and all too often, death.

In "Blood on the Coal", he opens a door into that darkened, alien world and shares the hardships and suffering of all who labour underground.

BLOOD ON THE COAL

There's blood on the coal.
God, there's blood on our coal:
For in it, I see
A working man's soul,

One of many
Who toil so well
In a world so close
And akin to Hell.

But the coal in his blood
Did him no good.
He lived and died
As hard as he could,
With lungs and breath
As black as the pit
That made him afraid,
Even to spit.

And for this human mole,
The only parole
While digging the hole
That became his last
Was the searing, white heat
Of a gas leak blast.

To the earth he belonged
And is now ever bound
As they lower what's left
Back under the ground.

Now his sons prepare
To join those in the mine
Who survived but to die
Another time.
While their days all choke
On ashes and coke
As the fruits of their labour
Go up in black smoke.
Leaving just ashes,
Exhausted and grey:
Like them, burned out
And then thrown away.

Oh, would that the earth
Gave her treasure away
But the like of these man
Forever must pay,
To warm colder hearts
While she takes her toll
On those who know well
That there's blood on the coal.

Poem reproduced by kind permission of Tony's family.

SNAP DECISION

Barney and Tommy sat in the manhole at snap-time.

"By gum, tha's lookin' reet wore out. What's up wi' thee? asked Barney.

"Wish I knew, came the reply. "When I lie on me bed at neet, me right leg shoots straight up in th'air an' t'other stays flat on t'mattress. Then a bit later, me left leg shoots up in th'air an' t'right 'un stays flat.:'

"Mun be real uncomfortable for thee" observed Barney.

"Tha can say that again," Tommy agreed and went on "Mind thee, I manage t'nod off after a couple of 'ours but t'missus tells me I keep doin' it in me sleep."

"Tell thee what, lad," Barney advised. "Go an' see t'doctor toneet cos e'll soon sort thee out."

The following day, the two met up in the manhole.

"What did t'doctor say then?" asked Barney.

"'e gave me a reet goin' o'er and said there were nowt wrong. Then afore I left, 'e said it were 'ereditary. Summat t'do wi' me genes. Reckons I gorrit from me Dad."

"'ow come?" asked Barney.

'e were a signalman on t'railway, tha knows," Tommy replied.

D. Hollows

SELFLESS DEVOTION

During my early days as a Bevin Boy, I noticed that many miners carried on their persons, slips of notepaper and pencils. I assumed correctly that in certain cases, they were used to record output but I also learned from a collier friend that they had an alternative purpose.

In a calm, matter-of-fact way, he explained "Well, son, should summat untoward 'appen down 'ere an' if our luck were to run out, we'd be able to write notes to our families tellin' 'em we love 'em and then we'd 'ope somebody finds 'em an' deli vers 'em".

An article written by Chris Lloyd of the 'Northern Echo' and here reproduced by his kind permission reads: "The most poignant tale of all though is of a miner trapped underground by an explosion at Seaham in 1871. He had time enough to scratch a letter to his wife onto the surface of his metal water-bottle. 'Dear Margaret, There was 40 of us altogether at 7a.m. Some were singing hymns but my thoughts was on my little Michael that him and I would meet in Heaven at the same time. Dear wife, farewell. My last thoughts are about you and the children. Be sure and learn the children to pray for me. Oh, what an awful position we are in.'"

On Wednesday, the 18th September 1880 at 2.20a.m., 164 men and boys lost their lives at the same colliery. Displayed in a local church a length of timber retrieved from the mine is displayed. It contains a message from one of the doomed men: "The Lord has been with us. We are all ready for Heaven. Bless the Lord. We have had a jolly prayer meeting. Every man ready for Glory. Praise the Lord. Ric Cole, half past 2 o'clock, Thursday".

There was to be found courage of the highest order from men who accepted that their earthly time was almost spent but whose thoughts were with those they held most dear, Facing death, they felt secure in the knowledge that God awaited them.

It is small wonder that I felt privileged and proud to work with such compassionate brothers who lived every minute, every hour and every day with deep faith and trust in their fellows and with little thought for themselves.

D. Hollows

WHEN DISASTER STRIKES (A FEW OF THE MANY)

Over the years and through various mishaps, thousands of miners, horses and ponies have lost their lives or sustained serious injuries underground. That dark world was filled with many hidden dangers and the greatest enemy was methane (firedamp) which seeped from the coal and rock fissures. It was lighter than air and would build up along the roof of the workings. When mixed with air, it could explode. The practice of stone-dusting helped to control it but when an explosion occurred, the results were catastrophic. In an instant, a whole district could be decimated and all human and animal life therein. For anyone who might survive the initial blast, there were the attendant threats of afterdamp (carbon monoxide) and choke damp (carbon dioxide).

The tragedy at the Wood Pit, Haydock, stands as the most disastrous in the area. In 1878, a massive explosion took the lives of two hundred men and boys and numerous ponies.

As a result, ninety-three wives were widowed and two hundred and eighty-two children orphaned. Among the dead was a father and his five sons, the youngest aged fourteen years. The colliery manager displayed outstanding courage by going underground and rescuing between twenty and thirty miners. It took several weeks to recover the bodies of the victims.

There have been many similar disasters within the industry and heavy losses inflicted on both men and animals. Indeed, they occurred so frequently that in certain areas, editors instructed staff not to report any further incidents as to do so might well have a demoralising effect upon the community.

TRIMDON GRANGE, TUDHOE AND EAST HETTON COLLIERIES

In February, 1882, sixty-eight men and boys died in an explosion at the Trimdon Grange Mine in County Durham.

Two months later and but four miles distant from Trimdon, an explosion in the Tudhoe Mine killed thirty-five miners. Sixty-nine of the eighty-six horses and ponies working in the pit were also lost.

A torrent of water poured into the East Hetton Mine, Kelloe, in May, 1897 and ten men were drowned. In true mining tradition, acts of great courage were performed by the searchers and by one man in particular, John Morley.

The tragedies at Trimdon Grange and Kelloe prompted Tommy Armstrong to record the incidents in verse and are reproduced by kind permission of his grandson, Ray Tilly.

THOMAS (TOMMY) ARMSTRONG

Thomas Armstrong, the second son of Timothy and Mary Armstrong, was born at Wood Street, Shotley Bridge, in August, 1848. When he was nine years' old, he began working in the mines as a "trapper boy" and lived for most of his life in the village of Tanfield Lea.

At the age of sixteen years, he began to write poetry for which he became well known throughout County Durham. It wasn't long before he was referred to as 'The Pitman Poet', the 'Tanfield Poet' and the 'Bard of the Durham Coalfield'. Perhaps his most celebrated poem is 'Nanny's A Maisor'.

Many of his works were set to music and are still sung today by various folk groups.

On Christmas Day, 1869, he married Mary Ann Hunter in Gateshead and they had fourteen children.

During his lifetime, he was a colourful character and was recognised wherever he went.

In later years, his health began to fail and he suffered a series of strokes. Residing in Tanobie and at the age of seventy-two years, he passed away in 1920.

Permission to reproduce information regarding Tommy's life and two of his poems has been kindly granted by his grandson, Ray Tilly.

Photograph courtesy of Ray Tilly

THE PITMAN'S POET (1848 – 1920)

TRIMDON GRANGE EXPLOSION

Let us not think of tomorrow
Less we disappointed be:
All our joys may turn to sorrow,
As we all may daily see.
Today, we may be strong and healthy
But how soon there comes a change,
As we may learn from the explosion
That has been at Trimdon Grange.

Men and boys left home that morning,
For to earn their daily bread.
Little thought before that evening
That they'd be numbered with the dead.
Let us think of Mrs. Burnett,
Once had sons but now has none,
By the Trimdon Grange explosion,
Joseph, George and James are gone.

February left behind it
What will never be forgot,
Weeping widows, helpless children
May be found in many a cot.
Homes that once were blessed with comfort,
Guided by a father's care,
Now are solemn, sad and gloomy,
Since the father is not there.

Little children, kind and loving,
From their homes each day would run
For to meet their father's coming,
As each hard day's work was done.

Now they ask if father's left them:
Then the mother hangs her head,
With a weeping widow's feelings,
Tells the child that "father's dead."

God protect the lonely widow,
Help to raise each drooping head,
Be a Father to the orphans:
Never let them cry for bread.
Death will pay us all a visit,
They have only gone before.
We may meet the Trimdon victims
Where explosions are no more.

Thomas Armstrong

Ray informs me that this poem has been published on numerous occasions.

KELLOE DISASTER

Death has paid another visit to some miners while below,
At a place they call East Hetton, little o'er five weeks ago.
Thirteen miners, strong and hearty, left their homes the sixth of
May,
Little thinking death was waiting soon to take their souls away.

It was on the Thursday evening when those miners did descend,
For the bread of life to labour, far from home and earthly
friends
They, like all good-hearted miners, each commenced to labour
free.
All was right till Friday morning-until shortly after three.

Then, alas, a rush of water burst into the mine below
And took those men away before it, any way it chose to go.
A deputy, the name of Morley, had descended underground
To examine working places: there, he heard a rumbling sound.

He shouted to the men to "Hurry, look for nothing, don't
delay."
As he spoke, the water caught him, he was nearly washed away.
There he saw two workmen struggling-to save them there was

little hope.
The only way that he could help them was to cast to them a rope.

He knew his life was in great danger, yet he could not pass these two:
He cast a rope and they both caught it. Then John Morley pulled them through.
Quite exhausted, wet and suffering, they were drawn from underground
How did they escape from drowning, people wonder all around.

To this noble-hearted hero, there is every credit due.
On the brink of death he ventured, such a noble act to do.
The masters of East Hetton Colliery and the working men around,
All should honour noble Morley for his bravery underground.

There were still eleven miners, hid from friends, entombed below.
None expected to be living but it did not happen so:
While a batch of men undaunted were exploring down below,
They heard a voice come from the water which encouraged them to go
Onward, they kept persevering, going along the engine-plane,
Travelling to the waist in water, when they heard a voice again:
A few more steps and then John Wilson by those gallant men was found.
Only they can tell their meeting in the water underground.

The exploring party took him in their arms uplifted high,
Bore him gently from the water to a place where it was dry.
From below, they soon ascended, attended to by skilful men.
Now John Wilson is recovering, which leaves the number drowned at ten.

Ten brave-hearted men of labour became victims underground.
A week elapsed before nine bodies by those gallant men were found.
James Oliver was still a-missing, lifeless in the mine below.
Men of bravery found the body on the 26th of May.
May the widows and the children who have lost their earthly friend,
Trust in God and He will guide them through all trials to the end.

And when earthly toils are ended, may they meet on Canaan's shore
With those victims of East Hetton: where, disasters are no more.

Thomas Armstrong

Ray advises me that his grandfather's poem has not appeared in print since its' publication in the Consett Chronicle, dated 11th June, 1897.

As a point of interest, John Wilson whose name appears in the poem was initially recorded among those drowned but mercifully, after four days underground, he was rescued.

MAYPOLE COLLIERY, ABRAM, NEAR WIGAN

August 2008, was the centenary of the Maypole Colliery explosion which took the lives of seventy-five men and boys. The pit headgear was completely destroyed and the shock waves were felt for miles around.

A rescue party was hastily organised. The mine was filled with toxic fumes and the rescuers quickly became exhausted but after being revived, they returned underground to resume their searches. In true mining tradition, there was no shortage of men to offer their services.

The scene that met them was one of utter devastation. The burned bodies of miners and pit ponies lay all around. Some looked as if they were sleeping while many others were unrecognisable.

Millions of gallons of water were pumped down the shaft and this triggered off a series of explosions as powerful as the initial one. For weeks, fires raged through the workings.

In mining areas, one is only too well aware of a strong corporate spirit. They are tightly-knit communities and Abram was and still is, no exception and scarcely a household remained unaffected.

On the 17th August, 2008, the monument under which some of the victims lie was re-dedicated. Church services, exhibitions, processions and a variety of associated activities were organised to honour those lost.

It was reassuring to see local schoolchildren involved in the proceedings, thus maintaining the tradition of reverence for those who had sacrificed their all.

There can be no doubting the fact that to think of men and innocent animals losing their lives in such horrific circumstance is heart-rending.

It is a blessing that nowadays, with the closures of most mines, such calamities have virtually been eliminated. In the few that still operate, greatly improved technology will minimise most risks.

Those who remain should ensure that future generations are made aware of the sacrifices made by miners, horses and ponies throughout the ages and that they are never forgotten.

D. Hollows

BURNS PIT, STANLEY, COUNTY DURHAM

There was an explosion at the Burns Pit in Stanley on the 16th February, 1909 which caused the biggest single loss of life in County Durham during the 20th Century. One hundred and sixty-eight miners were killed from either the force of the explosion, burns or the inhalation of toxic gases. The bodies of two of the men were discovered by accident some twenty years later. Many of those lost were young teenagers. Only thirty-four of the shift's workforce survived, as did some of the pit ponies.

When news of the disaster spread, people rushed to the mine and eventually, five thousand gathered at the pit-head awaiting news. At the time, a specialist rescue team was unavailable and fourteen hours elapsed before the first survivors were brought to the surface. Among them, was Frank Keegan, the grandfather of football legend, Kevin. Undaunted, he joined a party of searchers and returned underground.

A very brave midwife, Susanna Todd, also went into the mine to tend the injured and dying. On a poignant note, it was reported that some of the trapped men could be heard singing the hymn 'Lead Kindly Light'. Thanks to that gallant band, all of whom put their own lives at risk to save others, some miners made good their escape. The heroism of Frank, Susanna and their colleagues will forever be remembered in County Durham.

This year marks the centenary commemoration of the tragedy. A service will be held at the site, during which the 'Last Post' will sound and the bells of a nearby church will be rung 168 times while members of the community will observe a two minutes' silence.

As with many similar events in the various coalfields, local children will be involved. Groups of them will attend a service at the Beamish Mining Museum where they will participate in the hymn singing. It will be a very moving moment for those present as they watch the children reverently placing remembrance roses on the photographs of the victims, many of whom were but a few years older than themselves.

MARY N. BELL

Revealing a great sense of humour, Mary observed, "Obviously, I was fated to become a nurse for I bear my mother's maiden name of , Nightingale , and that says it all."

She exemplifies that vast, unheralded band of women whose lives were committed to supporting their mining menfolk, resolute and steadfast, through halcyon days and periods of great tragedy which were frequent.

So often, their daily routines must have be been overshadowed by apprehension, deep anxiety and foreboding over the safety of family members who laboured in dark and dangerous conditions.

During times of disaster, they were pillars of strength to those less fortunate. As with the miners, they too, were a race apart and Mary is truly one of that number.

She comes from generations of miners. Her paternal grandfather a deputy at the Black Prince Colliery, was severely injured underground and although he was rescued and brought to the surface, little could be done to save him and sadly, he succumbed. It was even more devastating for the family when shortly afterwards, his widow died, reputedly of a broken heart.

After World War Two, Mary corresponded with Peter Dickens, captain of the vessel Blencathra on which her late husband had served. Aware of her literary talent, Peter, a descendant of Charles Dickens, encouraged her to take up writing. He was obviously an astute man who inherited his forebear's perceptive skills.

Throughout the years, Mary has participated in numerous mining events. She is steeped in her community's customs and traditions and speaks with authority.

On a number of occasions, she has appeared on television and radio programmes. She is gifted in that she can express her thoughts and emotions in verse, an activity which she thoroughly enjoys. In deference to all whose roots are embedded in the mining industry, I consider it fitting to record a small selection of her many literary contributions.

PITMAN BEWARE

I dominate this place and you revolve around me,
Mesmerised, hypnotised, you are drawn to see
If I am a dream or a constant nightmare:
It is no hallucination, I am there.
Step into the cage, at the ring of a bell,
Plummet through the earth to a special Hell.
If I wish, I'll do you harm,
I'll break a limb, a leg or an arm.
Respect me or I'll take your life,
Make your child an orphan, a widow your wife.
Breathe in my stench, gases and dust.
Dig and get coal from my seams if you must
But pitman beware, you have one life to lose
And I will take it whenever I choose.

Mary N. Bell

EASINGTON COLLIERY, CO. DURHAM

Mary N. Bell
Easington Writers' Group
Easington Colliery, Co. Durham

Even before the official opening of Easington Colliery in 1910, the mine claimed its first victim in 1904 when the shaft was being sunk. Robert Atkinson, a fifty-six year old sinker, was buried in quicksand and his body was not recovered until over four years later.

At various times between 1910 and its closure in 1993, the mine claimed the lives of 180 men and boys due to various accidents. But it was on the 29th May, 1951, that the single loss of life was recorded. There was an explosion in the Five Quarter Seam, known as the Duck Bills when there were two shifts of men in the district. In all, eighty-three miners were killed.

On the morning of the disaster, a collier's wife stood at the front gate awaiting the return of her husband. She had carefully prepared his dinner and was concerned that he had not appeared. She was completely unaware that there had been a tragedy. Everyone at the pit-head was so intent on engaging in rescue work that there was little time to inform her of the event. Her husband did not return and she later learned that he had been one of the victims.

After extensive searches, Mary who for many years, had maintained close contact with Easington and its community, has produced a comprehensive list of the casualties at the mine. Because certain personal details are included, the lost become much more than mere numbers. One feels able to identify with each and everyone of them as though they were family, friends or neighbours. All of those men and boys emerge as immortal, vibrant souls whose suffering serves to remind us of the true cost of coal. Lists such as this, recording the names of so many casualties in a single mine, were repeated time after time throughout our coalfields.

EASINGTON PIT OPENED 1910 CLOSED MAY1993
Men and Boys killed

No	Name	Age	Occupation	Date killed	Details (if any)
1.	Robert Atkinson	56	Sinker	1904	While sinking the shaft was buried in quicksand 28th Nov.1904 body recovered 18th Feb 1909.
2.	Thomas Moseby	22	Hewer	24.7.1912	Killed
3.	John W. Nichol	23	Screener	19.8.1913	Killed
4.	Jack Lambton			20.11.1913	Fell off South pit engine house
5.	George Robinson	44	Hewer	3.4.1914	Killed
6.	George Lambton		Traffic Manager	4.12.1914	Killed by Loco
7.	William Hardy	45	Hewer	14.12.1914	Killed by fall of stone
8.	Owen Owens	30	Hewer	14.2.1916	Killed by fall of stone
9.	John Neasham 5,2nd Street East	48		23.3.1916	Killed
10.	Robert Ridley	19	Putter	17.9.1916	Killed
11.	Abraham Wayman	22	Hewer	2.10.1916	Killed
12.	Robert Herring	42		5.3.1917	Killed
13.	Edward Bowman	42	Stoneman	24.6.1917	Killed
14.	Richard Merritt 4,6th Street North	44		0.7.1917	Killed
15.	Patrick Gilmore 24, Station Road	22	Hewer	13.9.1917	Injuries lifting a tub
16.	Thomas Morris	15	Driver	26.10.1917	Killed
17.	J.W.(N) Raper	18	Engine lad	25.11.1917	Killed at 3rd West Low Main Seam
18	Thomas Mothersill 85, Station Road	20		1917	Killed at 2nd North Main Coal Seam
19	William Bel 6,5th Street North	52	Hewer	4.7.1918	Killed by fall of stone at East Flat Hutton Seam
20	Jos. Vickers 13,13th Street North	15		23.9.1918	Killed
21	Robert Todd	55	Hewer	31.10.1919	Struck on head by piece of stone
22	J.C.Robson	19	Labourer on screens	13.3.1920	Through a fall
23	John Pearce	56	Hewer	14.3.1920	Caught by a set while dressing
24	Allan Hocking	19		4.5.1920	Killed at Low Main Incline Hutton Seam
25	John G. Carter	22	Putter	14.7.1920	Fall of stone
26	Stephen Kirk	67	Stoneman	18.9.1920	Fall of stone
27	Joseph Sennet	23	Stoneman	31.8.1921	Fall of stone
28	John Tulip	48	Hewer	8.12.1921	Fall of stone
29	John Robert Robson	16	Landing lad	2.7.1922	Crushed by set
30	John Tulip	20	Putter	17.12.1923	Was found lying unconscious i.e. dead on travelling way
31	J.Ellwood		Deputy	27.10.1925	Run over
32	M. Leadbitter	52	Timber drawer	10.3.1926	Roof fall
33	T. Meakin	14 ½	Landing boy	21.3.1927	Died from accident. Caught by set

35	T.B. Grieves	27	Cutter	18.5.1927	Fall
36	M. Henderson	28	Hewer	31.8.1928	Fall
37	S. Jackson	14 ½	Shaft hand	21.2.1929	Caught by tubs
38	H. Bell	16	Landing boy	22.2.1929	Caught by set
39	J. Elland		Hewer	7.3.1929	Fall
40	G.G. Turner	15 ½	Engine boy	4.10.1929	Caught by engine
41	H. Wilson	36	Hewer	7.10.1929	Caught by set
42	Arthur Chambers	20	Haulage boy	13.10.1930	Caught by tubs
43	Thomas Simpson	24	Putter	29.2.1932	Found dead under tub of coal
44	Joseph James	33	Coal hewer	13.8.1932	Fall of stone
45	Albert Aitkenhead Lived at Horden	30	Stoneman	14.10.1932	Fall of roof
46	John Littler	25	Coal hewer	16.11.1932	Fall of stone
47	George Robert Barker	45	Coal hewer	13.4.1933	Fall of stone
48	Miles Handy	56	Stoneman	24.4.1933	Hit by fallen prop
49	William Robson	15	Datal lad	11.12.1933	Caught by set of tubs
50	Joseph Honour	45	Machine man	7.5.1934	Found under coal cutting machine
51	Elisha Potter	57	Canchman	13.11.1934	Fall of stone in return
52	S. Harris	25	Putter	15.12.1934	
53	M. Reilly	56	Stoneman	6.3.1935	
54	J.H.Morton	27	Driller	15.1.1936	Fall of stone
55	William Dunn	53		13.2.1936	
56	Anthony Gray	36	Filler	17.3.1936	Fall of rumble
57	Ernest Watson	38	Conveyor man	5.10.1936	Found gassed in the inbye side of a fenced off place
58	A.B.Cairns	34	Timber drawer	23.12.1936	Caught by fall of stone
59	R.N.Whinning	45	Hewer	1.8.1937	
60	James B. A. Raper	63	Wasteman	24.9.1937	Presumed hit by tubs
61	K. Goodwin	34	Hewer	21.10.1937	Fall of stone
62	Lancelot Turnbull	44	Hewer	22.11.1937	Fall of stone
63	Geo. B. Whiting	32	Stoneman	22.11.1937	Fall of stone
64	John Golightly	47	Hewer	2.2.1938	Fall of stone
65	James A. Daglish Westmoreland	34	Stoneman	16.12.1938	Struck with a prop that was knocked out by a piece of stone in return airway
66	Wm. Robinson	56	Shaftman	2.2.1940	Working in shaft on cage when it made a move and he lost his balance and fell off cage down shaft
67	Thomas Wheatley Collingwood	27		14.10.1940	Crushed by tubs at separation doors while operating clip
68	Daniel Ward	48	Timber yard worker	3.7.1941	Fractured finger while carrying a 7 foot prop died as a result of Tetanus 16.7.1941
69	James Williams	40	Surface labourer	23.1.1942	Crushed under lift at bank
70	Clifford Scott	41	Drawer	20.10.1942	Fall of post stone while drawing a bord (this is the spelling I found in the records should it be board I wonder)
71	Evan Ames	50	Coal hewer	23.10.1942	Fall of roof at the face of lift
72	G.W. Elliott	50		29.7.1944	
73	John Holden	43	Shifter	29.9.1944	Fall of roof

74	John Bee	72	Surface labourer	26.3.1946	Fell from gantry while tightening up hydraulic ram glands
75	George Goodrum	31	Hewer	26.4.1946	Found under first tub of four while putting
76	J.H.Robinson	42		12.6.1946	Run over by men riding set of tubs
77	W. Powers	38	Stoneman	25.9.1946	Lifting tub
78	Arthur Jones Lived at Wheatley Hill	34	Shifter	16.12.1947	Crushed between tub and timber tram
79	Joseph Deighton	25	Pony putter	8.1.1948	Injured by tubs in landing

DISASTER May 29th 1951

An explosion occurred in the FIVE QUARTER SEAM known as THE DUCKBILLS at 4.35am. when there were two shifts of men in the district. 38 belonging to 10 o'clock shift (stoneman shift) and 43 to 3.40am. (foreshift).

THESE ARE THE NAMES OF THE MEN KILLED.

80	John Anson	64	Shifter		
81	William Armstrong	55	Datal		
82	Mark Smart Bedding	38	Filler		
83	Matthew Blevins	27	Filler		
84	George Brenkley	20	Filler		
85	Thomas Brenkley	32	Filler		
86	Louis Brennan	49	Stoneman		
87	George Miller Brown	50	Datal		
88	Bertram Burn	25	Filler		
89	Emmerson Cain	63	Stoneman		
90	Frederick Cairns	23	Filler		
91	George Calvert	50	Stoneman		
92	James Calvin	51	Conveyor maintenance		
93	Frederick Carr	50	Electrician		
94	George William Carr	45	Timber drawer		
95	James Carr	38	Timber drawer		
96	John Edwin Challoner	53	Deputy		
97	Richard Champley	43	Cutter		
98	Albert Kerr Chapman	44	Stoneman		
99	Joseph Charlton	42	Master Shifter		
100	John Clough	57	Shifter		
101	William Arthur Dryden	27	Filler		
102	John Ellison	19	Datal		
103	Charles Fishburn	54	Shifter		
104	Henry Fishburn	23	Filler		
105	Thomas Garside	20	Datal		
106	Joseph Godsman	41	Cutter		

107	George Goulburn	57	Mason's labourer		
108	Albert Gowland	51	Deputy		
109	Ernest Goyns	60	Stoneman		
110	Herbert Goyns	56	Stoneman		
111	John Harker	53	Shifter		
112	John William Henderson	56	Shifter		
113	Thomas Heppell	31	Filler		
114	Daniel Hunt	54	Datal		
115	Stephen Hunt	24	Filler		
116	William Hunt	43	Datal		
117	Arthur Chambers Hutton	42	Filler		
118	Frederick Ernest Jepson	68	Shifter		
119	Lawrence Jones	36	Filler		
120	Thomas Edward Jones	35	Deputy		
121	Herbert Jeffrey Jobling	57	Shifter		
122	John Kelly	57	Datal		
123	William Kelly	28	Filler		
124	John Edward Armstrong Lamb	43	Datal		
125	Jesse Stephenson Link	44	Datal		
126	Joseph Fairless Lippeatt	37	Filler		
127	Peter Lynch	20	Filler		
128	Denis McRoy	23	Filler		
129	William James McRoy	31	Filler		
130	Robert William Milburn	26	Filler		
131	Harold Nelson	49	Stoneman		
132	Albert Newcombe	67	Stoneman		
133	Norman Nicholson	29	Filler		
134	Robert Noble	45	Shifter		
135	William Parkin	24	Filler		
136	William Edward Forbes Parks	62	Shifter		
137	Robert Pase	63	Shifter		
138	Stanley Peaceful	37	Stoneman		
139	Alexander Penman	42	Cutter		
140	James Porter	32	Filler		
141	John Thomas Porter	23	Filler		
142	Thomas Valentine Rice	53	Shifter		
143	John Robinson	50	Shifter		
144	John George Robson	25	Filler		
145	George Scott	53	Datal		
146	Albert Seymour	64	Datal		
147	Frederick Sillito	52	Shifter		
148	George Henry Stubbs	60	Shifter		
149	Hugh Bell Surtees	36	Datal		
150	Matthew White Surtees	61	Shifter		
151	Lawrence Thompson	54	Datal		

152	Thomas Thompson	28	Underground Bricklayer		
153	Thomas Trisnan	43	Stoneman		
154	Robert Turnbull	64	Master Wasteman		
155	George Wilkie	63	Shifter		
156	Reginald Wilkinson	40	Stoneman		
157	Robert Willins	45	Foreoverman		
158	Matthew Williams	18	Datal		Fatally injured died same day
159	John Wilson	62	Hauling engineman		
160	Stephen Wilson	60	Shifter		
161	John Young Wallace	26	Back overman Rescue worker		Overcome by noxious gas same day
162	Henry Burdess	43	Deputy Rescue worker		Overcome by noxious gas 1st June 1951
163	Norman Eales	47	Surface Hand	6.4.1953	Injured by blow on head while climbing ladder out of stone bunker – died
164	Arthur Elliott	15	Surface Hand	19.5.1953	Head caught by lift gate which is raised by lift cage
165	Thomas S. Carr	27	Puller	16.7.1954	Fall of stone while drawing
166	Herbert S. Hall	47	Coal Cutter	14.9.1955	Fall of stone
167	J. Handy	23	Coal Filler	4.1.1956	Struck by overlapping coal knocked on to chain conveyor
168	George F. Harriman	43	Puller	18.10.1957	Fractured jaw, ribs and legs
169	Charles Dedman	42	Tippler Operator	26.12.1961	Found with head crushed between tippler and 3 ton mine car
170	T. McGoldrick	56	Diesel Tractor Driver	19.6.1965	Head trapped by tube and tractor. Ventilation tube was too low
171	George Hancock		Power Loader	22.5.1967	Trapped by girder caught by a fall of stone when drawing girder
172	J.A.Musgrove	23	Power Loader	20.1.1968	Head trapped between girder and top of machine in stenton
173	Billy Challoner	47		18.7.1969	Removing stage loader when roof began to work. A major fall in advanced heading at the stenton junction. Fall 26ft 9 inches E.W. 23ft N.S.10ft high
174	Robert Fenwick	48		18.7.1969	Same as above
175	Stephen Knapper	16	Surface Hand	15.6.1971	Killed
176	W. Morris	61	Banksman	18.4.1975	Killed
177	W. Hogg	19	Underground	15.8.1980	Killed
178	R. Frecker	21	Underground	1.12.1980	Killed
179	Jonathan White	32	Power Loader	14.3.1991	Roof Collapse

EASINGTON PIT DISASTER, 1951

Head bowed at the foot of the mass grave,
Atmosphere serene and quiet:
My mind zoomed instantly back to the past,
Imagination running riot.

May twenty-ninth, nineteen fifty-one:
Can you hear the clash of a gate,
As an unsuspecting pit lad checks,
He has his water-bottle and bait?

He glances back at his home,
Unaware of what lies ahead
Not knowing the echoing sound
Is his swansong, unsung, unread.

Pit baths, change clothes, catch cage
Travel rocky underground hills:
Eighty-one ill-fated coal getters
Walk to death in the North Pit Duck Bills.

The explosion rocked the pit:
Black killer dust, white-hot hell.
To add to the anguish of Easington,
Two rescuers perished as well.

Jim, Jack, Tom, Bill Joe,
Jesse, Peter, Bert and John,
George, Mattie, Steve, Fred, Hughie,
A few of the names that we mourn.

Names written on the memorial,
On the hill overlooking the sea,
Ensuring the disaster of Easington
Is forever preserved in history.

Accountants are able to reckon,
Politicians fight to control,
Argue prices, rates and profits:
Easington knows the cost of coal.

Mary N. Bell

Mary's framed poem is displayed in the Easington Colliery Welfare Hall.

DISASTER

I'm scared,
I'm trying not to cry,
I don't want my Dad to die.

I want our Jim to come back.
I'm worried about my uncle Jack.
I hope they're still alive
I hope they will survive.

I hate the pit!
I hate it!
Hate it!

I feel so lonely.
If only
I could see my Dad.
He's trapped down there
And I'm up here.

I hate the pit!
I hate it!
Hate it!

Someone's coming,
They're carrying something:
It's a body.
Someone's crying,
Someone's sighing,
Someone says she wants to die.

I hate the pit!
I hate it!
Hate it!

Here's another body.
This is my worst moment:
It's my Dad.

I hate the pit!
I hate it!
Hate it!

This moving poem was written by Mary Bell and two pupils from the Easington Colliery Primary School and refers to the disaster at Easington Colliery in 1951.
The emotions expressed have been experienced by so many children worldwide who throughout the history of coal-mining, have lost loved ones underground.

UNIVERSAL COLLIERY, SENGHENYDD, 1913

At 8.10a.m. on the 14th October, 1913, a massive explosion ripped through the workings. Four hundred and forty men and boys were lost. The force of the blast was so powerful that the banksman on the surface was killed and his companion badly injured. The headgear was completely wrecked and it wasn't until the second week of November that men were able to go underground to inspect the damage.

The tragedy in terms of loss of life stands as the worst in British mining history. There cannot be any doubting the fact that as with all coalfield disasters, there would have been many heroic acts displayed in those suffocating caverns.

The adage "Fact is stranger than fiction" was clearly proven a little later when a miner who was not working on that ill-fated shift, joined the Army and was transferred to France. During a gas attack, he noticed that a comrade did not have a protective mask.

Looking at the boy, he said, "You need this more than I do, lad. Here, take mine. My lungs are all but finished anyway." Amazingly, he survived the attack and returned safely home

where he remained until he passed away in the 1920's.
Through him, the heroism of those whose lives were spent in
choking dust and darkness, shone like a beacon on the battle
field. His action symbolised the miners' philosophy that a
colleague's life should be saved regardless of the cost to oneself.

BRING OUT YOUR DEAD
(The Senghenydd Disaster)

Bring out your dead.
Hear the pit hooter bawl.
The dawn of a new day, dying once more,
Dragging each victim out of bed,
As the sad sound of the last call
Trumpets on through the valley of the poor,
Awaking the conscience of all,
To sackcloth and ashes strewn on the floor.

Bring out your dead.
Paint a cross here once more,
To recall the time a young boy would tread,
Barefoot down those carpet-less stairs,
To open the latch of that pock-marked door,
Where pungent pit clothes were hidden from sight
In drab patterns of patch-worn squares
That hung stiff and corpse-like, shrouding the night.

Bring out your dead.
Let the lucky sleep late.
Friend and neighbour, husband, father and son,
Through the winding labyrinth led,
Each following the leader, one by one,
Into the catacomb, there to wait
Until the thread of life is spun
And then cut by that grim goddess of fate.

Bring out your dead.
In hush and silent prayer,
Out of those depths of anguish and dread,
Out of the darkness and despair,

Where, mourning her sons, a mother weeping,
Chokes back her grief with sob-stricken breath,
As time, like a thief, comes creeping,
Through the Valley of the Shadow of Death.

Bring out your dead
Out of that seething heat.
Then count them slowly, score upon score.
Reach out to them, row upon row
And cover them up on that cold slab floor.
Then count them again as the numbers grow,
From house to house and street to street,
Until time shall pass and the pain will be no more.

J. Anthony Rock

J. ANTHONY ROCK

Anthony was a miner for 30 years and was forced to retire due to ill-health.

As a young boy, during World War Two, he lived with his grandparents for a while and witnessed at first hand the price paid by so many who supplied the nation's coal. It must have been a traumatic experience for him to see the suffering of his grandfather who lay slowly dying before him from the effects of dust inhalation over the years.

Anthony's experiences throughout his life have made a deep impression on him and are recorded in his prolific output of verse which has become a poetic diary.

NO GREATER LOVE

Amidst the obscenities of war, many courageous acts have been performed. There were those who received due recognition from a grateful nation but all too often, deeds of heroism must have gone unreported for fate had ensured that there weren't any survivors and no man remained to become a messenger.

So it was with the miners whose war zones lay deep underground. We know that men risked and sometimes lost their lives to rescue their friends. It was a daily occurrence about which the general public knew little.

Recently, older miners who were trapped in a mine in America, gave a younger member who had a growing family, their oxygen supply. As sole survivor, he was spared to tell the tale and he is but one of countless numbers who have during the course of their labours, witnessed the true interpretation of self- sacrifice.

LYME COLLIERY, HAYDOCK, LANCS (1930 & 1949)

On the 26th February, 1930, an explosion at the Lyme Colliery killed five men and seriously injured twenty others. The death toll finally rose to thirteen.

The efforts of Dr Winifred Bridges, a young woman, who went underground to tend the injured, are still fondly remembered in Haydock today.

In 1949, there was a second explosion. For some weeks, work to seal off the No. 1 pit which was worked out, had been going on. The work was very hot and men employed in the task had been taken to hospital, suffering from heat exhaustion.

At 5.45 a.m. on 16th September, 1949, just as the night shift was going off duty, there was a terrific explosion which blew out a massive stopping, constructed of sand and cement.

The Mines Rescue Team from Boothstown was summoned and five men went down the pit. Two of them lost their lives.

A British Empire Medal and several George Medals were later awarded by His Majesty King George the Sixth to those men who had displayed outstanding courage.

Courtesy of Geoff Simm and Ian Winstanley, from their book 'Mining Memories'.

GRESFORD COLLIERY (1934)

In the early hours of Saturday 22nd September, 1934, an explosion occurred at the Gresford Colliery, near Wrexham, N. Wales.

The men were working a double shift so that they might attend a football match between Wrexham and Tranmere Rovers later that day. Indeed, many had gone underground with their wages and admission tickets in their pockets.

Two hundred and sixty-three miners were killed and three rescuers died later as a result of their injuries. Due to the toxic fumes and fierce fires that raged, it was impossible to recover all the bodies. Further searches were officially cancelled for it was decided that no one could be saved from the dreadful conditions below. The mine was finally sealed to become a tomb.

Memories of that fateful night were recalled by the daughter of a miner who was lost. "My Dad always cycled to the mine and as a young girl, I would stand on the doorstep and wave him off. On that particular night, he propped up his bicycle against the wall opposite the front door and began to inflate his tyres. Then he gazed over at us with a long, lingering look,

'What is wrong?' Mother asked, 'Why are you looking at us like that? "

'Oh, nothing, dear " he replied with a "Goodnight and God

bless", he rode off and that is the last I saw of my father."
Today, a memorial tablet stands over the spot. It was unveiled
by His Royal Highness, the Prince of Wales in 1982 and serves
as a permanent reminder of that terrible tragedy.

SNEYD COLLIERY, STAFFORDSHIRE (1942)

At 7.50am on the 1st January, 1942, the last big disaster in the Staffordshire Coalfield was recorded. An explosion in the Banbury Seam of Number 4 Pit caused the deaths of 57 men and boys, the two youngest being 17 and 15 years of age. It was a very well-organised pit with a highly qualified management team. Only that day, safety inspections had taken place. Nothing untoward had been noted. It would seem that the catastrophe was caused by a set of runaway tubs which ran down an incline and came to rest, piled up one on the other. The dust explosion then occurred.

One survivor stated that as he drew timber to the coal-face, he was enveloped in a thick, black cloud. A 64 year old miner who had spent 40 years in mining, was knocked off his feet by the blast. After clearing his throat of the choking dust, he fell to the ground in a faint and after recovering, crawled in total darkness to the safety of another seam and in view of his age, was regarded by his colleagues as a hero. Another survivor was killed two years later in a roof-fall.

A family who had moved from Scotland lost their father and a brother aged 17 years. Before going on the shift, one young man asked his mother to lend him a shilling until pay-day. The coin was later recovered from his body, returned to his mother and now handed down through the family as a grim reminder of that dreadful day and the loss of a loved one. Relays of rescue teams from other collieries were sent to assist in the recovery operation. When they surfaced, they hesitatingly gave accounts of the terrible sights they had witnessed. As one rescuer's daughter put it, "My father was away for two days. He left home as a 40 year old and returned looking like a 70 year old."

Clearance had to be implemented quickly for this was 1942 and there was an urgent demand for coal. Due to the fact that so much was happening in the various theatres of war, the tragedy received limited journalistic prominence nationally but reports were published in the Midlands' newspapers. The area suffered another blow when there was an air raid. A pit-head structure was damaged and hastily repaired. The ostler's house was also hit. A group of miners who had just surfaced immediately ran to the building which had been demolished. Without hesitation, they tunnelled through the debris to reach the occupants, a father and his son. The former survived but the latter was beyond aid. Wherever miners are to be found, they are characterised by their deep concern for others. To help those less fortunate is inherent in their make-up.

Without exception, they emerge as men of great courage and as heroes who should never be forgotten.

Mining's toll in one area:

Pit	Victims	Pit	Victims
Apedale	30	Jamage	6
Brymbo	30	Lycett	73
Bunker's Hill	43	Minnie	156
Diglake	75	Mossfield	60
Institute	25	Sneyd	57

REQUIESCANT IN PACE

With pride, we remember through our tears
Men, boys and ponies who lost their years,
In caverns deep beneath the ground,
Where courage and humour e'er abound.

Enshrouded in darkness, they laboured and toiled
And in fleeting moment, were cruelly encoiled
By a horror that seeping vapours make:
An endless risk all miners take.

Their day was done in that murky mine.
But from those depths, a light will shine
On caring souls with spirit sweet,
Now refreshed at our Saviour's feet.

Though years pass by and shadows fall,
We are surely embraced by the love of all
Who are never forgotten, never afar,
Finding Heaven's portals forever ajar.

A band of brothers and equine friends:
A sacred bond that never ends.
Together, they faced life's final test
And found their peace in eternal rest.

D. Hollows

THE DARKEST HOUR

Throughout the years, numerous underground disasters resulting in the loss of loved ones, have devastated thousands of families. Miners were only too aware of the dangers they faced as they toiled in those labyrinths and to resurface unscathed at the end of a demanding day's work was a bonus and a blessing.

Fatalities occurring on the surface which are mining related are comparatively rare but in 1966, there befell a tragedy which shocked our nation and indeed, the entire world.

For some time, there had been heavy rainfall which undermined a slag-heap overlooking a Primary school in Wales.

With ravaging effect, it began to move and gathered momentum as it finally engulfed the building, burying those within. In all, 144 souls perished. 116 of them were happy, innocent children, aged between 7 and 10 years. Rescuers did their utmost to release them but the chilling, black sediment had already taken its toll. Together, they now rest on a tranquil hillside which, as one gazes at the memorials, embellished by tears and memories, seems to touch the Heavens from whence they came and where they now dwell. In deep contemplation, one may for a brief moment, be blessed to hear the sound of childish laughter carried on the wind and echoing through the green hills and valleys. Then silence reigns once more.

Aberfan cannot and never will be forgotten for on that day, a young generation was lost. May they now live again in God's great Peace and may He ease the suffering of their grieving families.

ABERFAN

High on a hill, a man-made mound appears:
A manifestation that multiplied to spread
A malignant growth of tentacles fed
From the burrowed depths of bygone years,
Of toil and sweat, tenacity and tears
And higher still, the monster rears its head,
Incorporating the earth, the dust of the dead
And the village waits and watches and fears.

Some voices were heard, the danger was clear
But many were silent as poised for the kill,
The monster's huge body began to fill.
Some remained aloof, refusing to hear
The loud rumblings as the monster drew near,
 Its body becoming bigger, enormous, until
It toppled over and slid down the hill,
Devouring in its path all those held dear.

J. Anthony Rock

ABERFAN
THE SALVATION ARMY AT WORK

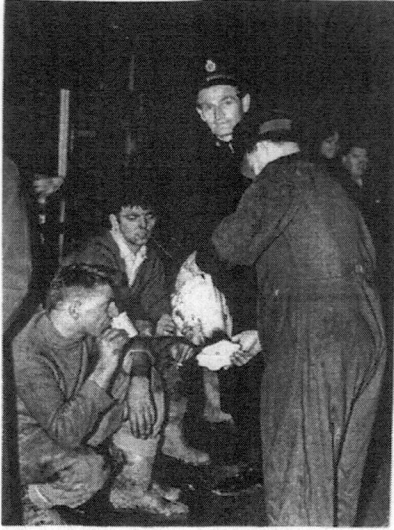

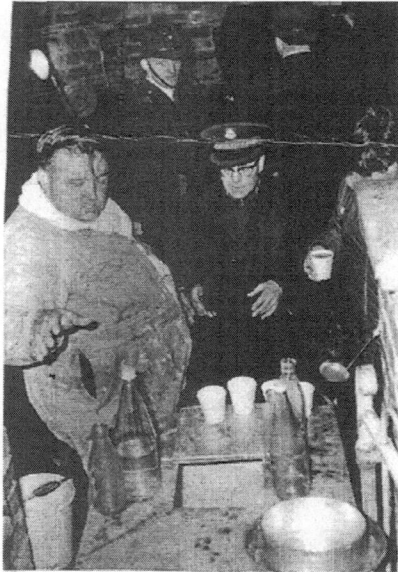

HEROES ALL

Photographs courtesy of The Salvation Army

THE DUKE OF EDINBURGH AT ABERFAN

AN APPRECIATION

At this point, it would be remiss of me not to acknowledge the contribution made by a group of heroes and heroines whose lives are dedicated to succouring those less fortunate. In war and in peace, they have made their presence felt and there are so many who have reason to be grateful to them.

Throughout the various coalfields, miners too were members of that group.

During the many underground tragedies, they were in attendance on the surface supplying food, drinks and comfort to the rescue teams and distraught relatives.

They carry out their duties quietly and efficiently and do not seek plaudits for their unwavering support. They will forever be honoured by members of the mining communities for they bring light from the darkness of disaster and despair. Long may the work of the Salvation Army continue.

D. Hollows

UNTO ETERNITY

Reet good it were to get off wom,
After sayin' "Good neet" to my best mate, Tom.
'e'd go one way. I'd go t'other:
Close we were, like brother an' brother.

I recall that day we went below
An' 'ad our snap in lamp-light glow.
'e' joked, I laughed. It were really great:
Best friend I 'ad, a smashin' mate.

Then off we went down th'aulage track.
I 'ad no idea e'd ne'er walk back.
We both took up our reetful place
In that narrer seam wi' glistenin' face.

A rumble comes from all around
An' thunderous echo, a warnin' sound.
Down come a fall o' sharded rock
An' I recoiled in sudden shock.

Recovered, I cradled young Tom's 'ead,
In chokin' air, so full o' dread,
To give 'im comfort, courage an' love
An' together, we prayed to our Lord above.

"Not to worry, owd lad", groaned my pal, Tom.
"I'm all reet now, t'pain's all but gone."
'e lay there still, life ebbin' away
I knew too well 'e could not stay.

Tom smiled, "We've been like brothers down the years.
No frettin' now. Go wipe thy tears.
Through the dark, it looks so bright,
Wi' kinfolk waitin' in dazzlin' light.

From time to time, just think o' me.
I won't be far away, tha'll see."
An' in my own life's eventide,
'e stands theer, smilin' by my side.

D. Hollows

To witness the loss of a colleague underground was a traumatic experience and such incidents occurred frequently throughout our coalfields.

BETWIXT AND BETWEEN

Alex Lawrence
Walsall Wood Pit

Twelve years ago, I came to live in a 16 storey block of flats on the ground floor. Every time that I see or hear that the lift is stuck, I think of the 22nd August, 1946. I was working at Walsall Wood Pit on the afternoon shift, waiting to go down. The banksman told us they were having trouble with the boilers. Both cages were ascending and descending but could not reach either the top or the bottom. After a while, a repair was effected. The under-manager said, "It's all right now, lads." Nine of us entered the cage to go underground but we all wished we hadn't. It went down about half-way and suddenly stopped. Then it started to go up and down like a yo-yo for about fifteen minutes. We hadn't any idea what was going to happen. Three or four times we managed to see the banksman's legs and shouted to him to take us further up the shaft so that we might get out. He replied that the boiler had broken down again. Again it went down and stopped just past half-way and there we stayed for between two and three hours. After a while, I began to eat my snap and joked to the other lads that I would save some of it for the following weekend. I wished I hadn't said it for the others in the cage began to moan and sigh for they had visions of being stuck there for days.

Finally, we arrived at the pit-bottom. The manager was standing there and said to us, "Right, lads. You can get off now," to which we replied, "We've had enough. We're stopping on" and back we went to the surface. Going across the bank, we met one of the Brownhill's fireman who had helped. I looked at him and said, "Thanks, mate!

A few years later, the cage crashed to the pit bottom and put us out of work for two weeks. We had to attend the pit every day to sign on. Some of the lads turned up in their best clothes and had a shock when they were told that the pit was operating again.

This story is reproduced by kind permission of Sheila Keates, the daughter of the contributor, Alex Lawrence.

Alex became a miner when he was 14 years of age and left in his early sixties, due to his suffering from pneumoconiosis which sadly shortened his life.

A STRANGE ENCOUNTER

Although every word of this story is true, there will be those who will claim that what I saw was nothing more than a figment of my imagination.

At the time, I was working on the foreshift which meant that no sooner had I dropped off to sleep than the alarm clock would ring at 2.00a.m. and after a quick bite to eat, I would set off for the pit.

One Autumn morning, I stepped outside my house and looked up at the clear, starry sky. A full moon had almost turned the darkness into daylight. At the end of the street stood the Miners' Reading Rooms and Institute, partially illuminated by a gas lamp attached to an outer wall. In the chill night air, I quickened my step as I headed toward the old, worked-out Auckland Park Colliery which was the picking-up point for our bus transport.

As I strode past the Institute, I became aware of an approaching figure, dressed in what appeared to be a white raincoat and wearing what was known as a 'pixie hat' which was a popular form of headwear among the ladies, particularly in wet weather. We were drawing closer to one another.

Suddenly, she stepped off the pavement and began to cross the road.

It was a weird experience for she seemed to float rather than walk and I could not see a pair of legs or a face. Instead, the form was enveloped in a bluish, hazy light and it became clear to me that I had been mistaken about the clothing for in reality, I had been looking at a nun's habit. Cautiously, I followed to get a closer look but in an instant, she had completely vanished.

For a long time afterwards, I was shocked and mystified by what I had witnessed and the more I thought about the incident, the more confused I became.

I must admit that I had been taken by surprise and did not feel unduly fearful for the apparition did not, in any way, appear to be malevolent.

Some time later, I moved to Aycliffe to live and to work. There, a free newspaper, the 'Newton News' was circulated and one day, my attention was drawn to an article which referred to the 'White Lady Ghost'

Apparently, between Aycliffe and Darlingon there was a nunnery. I then read that the body of a murdered nun had been discovered hidden under a hedge and that her murderer had never been identified. It was claimed that the ghost had been seen in the areas of Aycliffe, Rushyford and Auckland Park.

Years later, I read in my daily newspaper, the 'Northern Echo', that a driver had been travelling along the AI, an old Roman road. As he approached the Gretna Inn which is now a motel, he noticed a woman sheltering in the doorway for it was raining heavily. She wore what appeared to be a white raincoat and a 'pixie hat'. He stopped his car and waved to her, indicating that he would give her a lift. He opened the rear door and she stepped inside.

In response to his asking her where she wished to go, she pointed toward Rushyford, some three miles away. Upon arrival, he opened the door to let her out but she had disappeared. He thought it very strange for the doors were fitted with anti-child locks and could not be opened from the inside except by the driver. Concerned as to his passenger's whereabouts, he drove back along the road but there wasn't any trace of her. He then reported the incident to the police and appealed through the 'Northern Echo' for any relevant information but there was no response until a few weeks later.

A man riding a motor-cycle had stopped outside the Gretna Inn on a different date. He was aware of a female wearing a white raincoat and a 'pixie hat' standing at the same spot.

She accepted his offer of a lift as pillion passenger and pointed toward Rushyford. When he reached his destination, he stopped to let her alight but she had disappeared without trace, He was very shocked and was worried by the thought that she might have fallen off without his knowledge.

As with the car driver, he retraced his route but of her, there was no sign. He too, reported the matter to the police.

In this modern age, so many strange incidents can be explained away logically. However, there are those which seem to defy all rationale. If one chooses not to believe in ghosts, so be it. Speaking for myself I know what I witnessed on that Autumn morning long ago. How can I possibly be an unbeliever?

D. Fisher

LOOK ON THE BRIGHT SIDE

It's not all doom an' gloom down t'pit, tha knows.
We've 'ad a reet laugh o'er owd Tom's toes:
Well, wi' 'is nails, that is, I 'asten to say
An' 'e made up 'is mind only t' other day.

Wi'out scissors an' file, they'd grown real long,
So, 'ow could 'e cut 'em when they'd grown that strong?
'e 'opped an' 'e jumped like a man wi' fleas.
Done regular like, 'e'd 'ave 'ad more ease.

T'farrier will sort 'em, 'ave no fear.
'e's got steady 'ands when 'e's off the beer.
Nay, mate, 'e did Jim's las' week, tha knows.
Got rid o' t' nails an' some o' 'is toes.

I've thowt an' thowt for days on end.
Now they've grown through me clogs. I'm goin' round t'bend
Came an idea. "Gorrit", we 'eard 'im mutter.
"At th'end o' t shift, I'll trim 'em wi' t'cutter."

D. Hollows

TO HAVE AND TO HOLD

My father was buried under a fall of stone and received an injury from which he never fully recovered. First Aid at the colliery was primitive. There wasn't an ambulance available and it was decided that he should be carried home in a cart pulled by a pony. I felt very angry for it was winter and there was a ten mile journey ahead. Fortunately, a battered old car which was laid up for the duration of the war was found. Petrol was rationed but someone turned up with a drop. The car itself was used by the owner to shelter his hens and the interior was a complete mess. The car engine wheezed into life and off we went. Dad lay on the rear seat whilst I sat on the edge to ensure that he didn't fall off. We travelled up hill and down dale as the driver struggled to control the vehicle which didn't have any brakes. It was a hair-raising experience but I had to give credit to him for his skilful use of the clutch. The journey over, Dad received treatment and managed to survive.

Later, I too, was involved in an accident. As a Bevin Boy, I was working on a conveyor belt. I was wrestling with a big lump of grey-coloured coal. My job was to throw it down a chute into a wagon under the screens. It was then that I saw my finger which was bleeding profusely hanging off.

An old pit man took me to the colliery's lamp-room and

introduced me to the First Aider who was puffing away on a foul-smelling, short-stemmed clay pipe. Round his waist, he wore a filthy, black apron which matched the colour of his hands. Out came the bandages and the iodine and I had the biggest shock of my life. He took out his knife which he used to score his pipe and ran its blade back and forth through the flame of an oil-lamp. He told me that he was sterilising the blade so that he could amputate my finger. I asked him for a bandage, folded the torn digit in the palm of my hand and shot out of the lamproom but before leaving, I informed him that I was off home to see our family doctor, Dr Frazer to whom my mother gave tuppence a week as insurance. Using his skill, he saved my finger which remains as good as the others to this day, even though it is somewhat bent.

I was off work for about three months and when I returned, I had to restart my surface training. My experiences underground at a later date and in another mine, resulted in my becoming a fully-qualified First Aider. I always made sure that I carried a sharp, clean-bladed pocket-knife and of course, one that had never seen the inside of a pipe.

D. Fisher

SUPERSTITION

The Oxford Dictionary defines superstition as 'an idea or practice founded on increasing belief in magic or witchcraft and an irrational fear of the unknown or mysterious.' Rituals intended to thwart evil and to entreat the support of unseen benevolent powers have been performed by humans from time immemorial.

It is, in fact, man's acknowledgement of his own limitations and frailties as a member of our vast, complicated universe. We are all only too well aware of the many diverse methods employed in order to ensure good fortune.

The list is endless and there are millions of people worldwide who uphold such beliefs. It would take a foolhardy person to disparage these tenets as our protagonist, Fred, found to his cost.

SUPERSTITIONS

Superstitions were born with the advent of man,
Uncertain, unsure of creation's great plan.
Incantations and charms that all understood
Might thwart any evil and induce naught but good.

So many were soothed through this belief:
And good fortune was greeted with untold relief
But for one dissenter, by name of Fred,
Exclusion from custom held no dread.

"No new shoes on t'table an' coal at New Year?
Forget it lads, tha's got nowt to fear.
An' wha' abaht luck when tha sees a black cat?
Leave me out, mates. I can't 'old wi' that.

Wi' t'new moon, turn t'coins in thy pockets, they say
An' throw salt o'er thy shoulder, nay, no way.
To my thinkin', it's nowt but a waste:
Salt goes on t'grub to give it some taste."

With placard, defiant, he walked down the street,
Canvassing those he chanced to meet.
"It's rubbish, all rubbish," he cried aloud
To the puzzled faces in the crowd.

Under ladders propped up against a shop wall,
He stood, pressing his point to one and all
But that day, a sharp lesson was learned by Fred
When a tin of red paint crashed down on his head.

He's now a changed man, I hasten to say,
Obsessed by rituals, day by day.
For superstition's observance, he shows no constraint
And thanks are due to a tin of red paint.

D. Hollows

SUPERSTITIONS

In general, miners were no more superstitious than other members of society but in view of the nature of their work with its daily uncertainty and danger, there were a few observances that were peculiar to them. To go underground on New Year's Day was considered inadvisable and should a black cat cross the path of a collier on his way to work, the latter should return home forthwith for to report for duty could forebode ill. Many years ago, it was uncommon to encounter a female in the streets during the early morning as most miners' wives were confined indoors attending to domestic duties. To see one en route to the colliery served as a salutary warning and one should abandon all hope of joining the shift until the following day. Nowadays, had the mines been operating on the prolific scale of long ago, many would have ceased to operate overnight for with today's increase in female labour, thousands of working women now occupy our streets. If, on his way to the pit, a miner realised that he had forgotten an essential item, it indicated that he was not intended to report for duty that day. Finger and toe nails should never be trimmed on Fridays. To do so, would most certainly invoke the wrath of the Devil. Some miners would not sleep above ground floor level as this ritual ensured their safety and good fortune. A long-standing and popular myth which endured for years related to the miners' washing habits at the end of the shift. As one contributor observed, "A miner would never wash his back as he reckoned the soap and water weakened it.

As a young boy, I vividly remember my father getting bathed in the tin bath in front of the fire. When my mother washed his hair, she had to make sure no soap or water went on his back. When the pit-head baths were opened in my home village of Tanfield Lea, very few miners used them at first. It must have been a few years before they were fully used."

D. Hollows

A LANCASHIRE TALE

Many years ago, the only access available to miners on their way to a certain pit-head was a single road on which stood the local cottage hospital. About to join the day shift, it was not unusual for them to cross paths with a small group of uniformed nurses who after the night's work, emerged from the building. Upon seeing them, some of the miners would freeze in their tracks, turn round and immediately return home. To them, the presence of a nurse before a shift began was a bad omen and might forewarn of tragedy underground. Concern over the rate of absenteeism was expressed by the mine's manager and in order to solve the problem, a joint meeting between colliery management and the hospital authorities was arranged. Urgent steps had to be taken and after much discussion, the panel decided upon a most unusual course of action. It was agreed that the procedure of permitting the nurses to leave the hospital at the customary time must be maintained but with the proviso that they should change out of their uniforms before departing. Indeed, they were instructed to change into men's clothing. This, they did and the experiment was a success. Normal attendance at the mine was restored. Little did those who had formerly absented themselves from work realise that the "men" who hurried past them homeward bound and who had unwittingly created so much anxiety and apprehension were in fact, midwives.

READ THE INSTRUCTIONS (A TALE FROM THE COUNTY DURHAM COALFIELD)

Recently, I conversed with an acquaintance who informed me that both his father and grandfather had been miners. "My Gran recounted this tale to me when I was a young boy," he said and continued, "Grandad was quite a character. He was a collier and in those days, they did not have pit-head baths at his mine. As with so many others, he had to wash himself in a tub before the fire.

One day, he arrived home after the shift. His bath was already prepared for him. Of course, that was Gran's responsibility and woe betide Grandad if he returned home late. She would tell him off in no uncertain terms. Once stripped of his clothing, he would test the water temperature with his elbow and if acceptable, would hop into the tub and scrub himself."

"He wasn't one of those lads who didn't wash his back because he thought it might weaken him, was he?" I asked.

"No, nothing like that," came the reply," But he always complained that his skin was deeply ingrained by coal dust and that no amount of scrubbing would remove it. He would often say, "I'd give owt to feel really clean.'

On one occasion, Gran was in the kitchen making his tea and

Grandad was singing as he soaked himself. It would seem that as he sat there, his eyes wandered to the table in a corner of the room . On it, stood a bottle. It was obviously Gran's shampoo and being the sort who would try anything once, he picked up the bottle and emptied its contents into the water. Then he began to scrub himself again. Gran entered the room and noticed that the empty container was lying beside the tub. Grandad looked up and smiled at her. 'By gum, lass,' he said. 'I've never felt so clean in all my life. I reckon from now on, I'll be using that shampoo every time I have a wash."
'Shampoo, shampoo, what shampoo? she asked. 'That, my lad, is lavatory cleaner. So if you think it's that good, you'll have to scrub yourself in the privy from now on."
Gran's suggestion was never implemented. Two months later, when Grandad's all-over skin rash had disappeared, it was back to that firm favourite of all miners, carbolic soap."

D. Hollows

Photograph courtesy of D. Fisher

BEVIN BOYS OF GREAT BRITAIN

John R. Kitching
Brandon, Durham

When moves were being made to recognise the service of the Bevin Boys during the War years, I decided to produce a lapel badge to commemorate their invaluable contribution. The Durham miners very much appreciated their support.

I incorporated the words "Thanks! 60 Years On" which emphasised the length of time it had taken to honour them.

The badges were available at the Durham Miners' Gala in 2005 and for a minimal sum, were purchased by Bevin Boys who attended the event. I believe that they were worn by some of those who were invited to Westminster when the intention to award Veterans' Badges was publicised.

It was a great pleasure and a privilege to make a tangible token that was highly regarded by the Bevin Boys of Great Britain.

One of the many badges designed and produced by John

Members of my own family who worked in the mines could testify to the fact that the work was arduous and extremely dangerous. I well recall my grandfathers being presented with a retirement certificate by the National Coal Board for a lifetime of service underground and for the following two years, seeing his life ebbing away due to his dust-damaged lungs.

In view of the great sacrifices made by so many miners over the years, it would be a tribute to them if we could join together in seeking official approval for the initiation of a National Miners' Memorial Day when we might honour miners past and present.

The support of Bevin Boys would be most welcome and I wish continued success to members of the Association. My sincere regards to you all.

John

John is Chairman of the Browney Miners' Lodge Banner Group and Founder of the Durham Miners' Heritage Group. By organising exhibitions and giving lectures in local schools, he helps promote the mining heritage of County Durham. He is also an avid collector of mining memorabilia.

Footnote by D. Hollows

Recently, it came to my attention that a local widow, now in her eighties, whose late husband served as a Bevin Boy in the Notts. Coalfield, did not qualify for the Veterans' Badge Award. She is but one of a large number who are denied recognition for their partners' contribution to the War effort.

Non-gratis medals may be bought from several suppliers but for many senior citizens who may not have family members to help financially, the costs involved may well be prohibitive. After discussing the matter with some of my ex-miner friends, she was surprised and delighted to receive two badges and a box of flowers. As she is recovering from a stroke, these gifts were, in themselves, a therapy.

In true mining tradition, there were those who were only too willing to offer her their support. Her situation was not ignored and forgotten and thanks go to John Kitching and to Dennis Fisher for their kind consideration.

A SMALL SELECTION OF PETER'S ART WORK

Peter French
Bevin Boy, Houghton Pit, Houghton-le-Spring, Co. Durham

Photograph courtesy of Peter French

The Rt. Hon. Ernest Bevin addressing miners at the Durham Big Meeting, 26th July 1947.

Thou dis'nt swally it!...thou spits it out lad!
Sketch courtesy of Peter French

PAYING THE PENALTY
(The art of chewing tobacco)

HAM & EGGS IN THE CANTEEN   *1946*
Sketch courtesy Peter French

NEWSFLASH

PETER FRENCH 1947

High-definition scan of original watercolour by Peter French, 1947

TUB HEIGHT

THE PIT PONIES

Pit ponies in their stable lay
No bigger than some breed of dog,
Crunched and munched through bales of hay,
Then slept unmoved, like a log.

They'd pulled and pulled for a shift or more,
Weak with all the strain,
Shoulders skinned and sometimes raw,
They would surely feel the pain.

Some fine day when light is there,
Far from dust and grime,
Fresh green grass will be everywhere,
Even though they are past their prime.

Courtesy of Jack Thompson from 'Looking Back', his collection
of poems.

ALL TOGETHER NOW

When a country's survival is threatened, singing can be a boost to morale, forging and enhancing national unity in a common cause.

Throughout the ages, servicemen have sung many diverse ditties to elevate their spirits and to reinforce their sense of solidarity. Often, the words expressed, showed an acceptance of the inevitable and with it, a resolve to resist the intolerable regardless of the cost.

The Bevin Boys were no exception. Despite the reluctance of the majority who had volunteered for and in certain cases, been accepted for military service, they complied with official instructions and achieved what was expected of them.

THE BEVIN BOYS' SONG

We had to join, we had to join, we had to join old Bevin's
Army.
Three quid a week and b****r all to eat,
Hob-nailed boots and blisters on our feet.
We had to join, we had to join, we had to join old Bevin's
Army.
If it wasn't for the War, we'd be where we were before,
Bevin, you're b****y barmy.

DURHAM MINERS' GALA, 2004
ALL TOGETHER NOW

Photography courtesy of R. Fisher

Led by Warwick Taylor, M.B.E., Vice President of the Bevin Boys Association, a group of our members join in the protest song.

AYO GURKHALI, DURHAM MINERS' GALA, 2008

Photography courtesy A. Fulcher

Mid-ground. Dennis Fletcher hands over the Bevin Boys' Banner to his close friend, Penker, a Gurkha who is wearing the chain of office, displaying miners' identity discs.

Penker considered it a great honour to assume the role of banner bearer. His willingness to support the cause of the Bevin Boys symbolises the loyalty of these brave men to our nation.

It is gratifying to note that through the efforts of Joanna Lumley and so many others, their dedication has now been acknowledged. 'Ayo Gurkhali'.

GALA DAY

Wakened early by the sound of brass:
It was Gala Day and crowds would amass
On their way, trumpets blowing,
Banners waving, to the Gala going.

In the city, marching all abreast,
Their bands and banners by far the best.
Miners' families made up the crowd
As they stood to attention, very proud.

The cathedral stood, such a wonderful sight,
Over a hundred years, seen miners fight,
For an existence and the world to know
From Miners' Day, justice might flow.

Courtesy of Jack Thompson from 'Looking Back', his collection of poems.

REUNITED

The shift over, Ted and Charlie sat in the canteen enjoying a welcome cup of tea.

"What's make o' this?" asked Charlie as he rummaged in his jacket pocket and produced a crumpled scrap of paper. He went on, "I was 'avin' me snap in the old workings when I 'appened t'dig t'toe o' me boot in t'dust an' then I found this. It's signed by a Bevin lad an' I recall tha' was one o' 'em way back in t'war."

Ted straightened the creases and began to read aloud:

"So I'm a conchie, deserter, enemy agent and all And I got a white feather outside the dance hall. I couldn't care less about the first three of these But no more white feathers, folks: they just make me sneeze." Bevin Boy, 1944"

"What's all that about feathers?" queried Charlie. Ted smiled. "Well, this poem just about sums up what we had to put up with when we were youngsters."

"How does tha mean?" came the question.

"You will remember that we didn't wear uniforms like the other chaps in the Armed Forces. Most folk didn't know that we were doing our bit. Some thought we were conscientious objectors, deserters or even worse, enemy agents."

"Aye but what about them there feathers?" asked Charlie.

"Being given a white feather meant that you were nothing more than a coward," came the reply.

"That's a bit o'er t'top," interposed Charlie.

"Agreed," said Ted, "But the Bevin Boy who wrote this must have seen the funny side. He had a job to do so he got on with it, nothing more, nothing less."

"Looks as if 'e were allergic to feathers, an' all. Did tha ever get one?" Charlie asked.

"Only one and that was enough," Ted answered.

"Made me sneeze until the tears ran."

"Wonder what 'appened to t'lad who wrote them words?" Charlie pondered. "

"You're looking at him," Ted replied with a smile.

"Well, I never," exclaimed a bemused Charlie.

The last Bevin Boys were demobilised in 1948 under the same time-scale as that which applied to members of the Army. Unlike their counterparts in the Armed Services, their contribution to the war effort was not acknowledged. They did not receive gratuities, replacement suits or medals and in many cases, reinstatement to their pre-war occupations was not guaranteed. It is small wonder that they were known as the "Forgotten Army".

In 1989, the Bevin Boys' Association was formed in the Midlands and had only thirty-two members. Since those early days, membership has increased considerably and one is afforded an opportunity to maintain and extend the spirit of comradeship that existed during the 1940's. Representatives now attend various festivals and galas which are mining orientated.

In 1995, they participated in the VE and VJ Day Fiftieth Anniversary commemorations and were finally permitted to take part in the Cenotaph March Past. Until recently, membership of the Royal British Legion was denied them but they are now accepted as associate members.

It wasn't until 2008 that they were represented at the Albert Hall Service of Remembrance and were awarded Veterans' Badges by the Government.

D. Hollows

TRUTH WILL OUT (OVERHEARD IN THE HOSTEL)

Many Bevin Boys who were conscripted had set their hearts on joining the various Armed Services and voiced their objections to being directed into the mines at tribunals which were set up in a number of areas.

The main difficulty lay in the protesters being able to present plausible reasons for their opposition. Perhaps the most common excuse is contained in the following anecdote.

After a tiring shift at a nearby colliery, two newly-arrived Bevin Boys returned to the hostel and feeling extremely fatigued, threw themselves on to their respective bunks.

"Had a good day?" asked Tim.

"Not too bad," Andy replied.

"You sound like a local lad," Tim observed.

"Right first time. I'm Lancashire born and bred and I'm proud of it. And where are you from then?" Andy questioned.

"Devon. You know, where they make real clotted cream and cider that's out of this world. I must say, I really miss it. Never thought I'd land up in a coal-mine though I wanted to join the Navy. Was even in the Cadets for two years. Then my number came up."

"Mine too," Andy agreed. Wanted to join the R.A.F. myself, I even went before a tribunal and when they asked me why I didn't want to go underground, I told 'em I had claustrophobia. Trouble was, there were eight other lads there and they all had the same excuse. Turned us all down, of course. "

At that, Tim burst out laughing. "My excuse was the same as yours", he said. "Reckon I put on a pretty good act. I said I couldn't stand being shut in, couldn't breathe and was likely to pass out. I sat there rolling my eyes and making my body shake. They were so concerned that one chap got me a glass of water and one old lady waved a bottle of smelling salts under my nose. Although I say it myself, Andy, I was a class act. I had 'em all in the palm of my hand and knew I had cracked it when the chairman said, 'In view of your reaction, young man, it would appear that the mine is not for you. Just as a matter of interest, which branch of the Royal Navy do you wish to join?' 'Done it, done it' I thought to myself. Then I dropped a right clanger."

"Why, what did you say?" Andy asked.

"Like an idiot, I replied, 'The Submarine Service, sir'"

D. Hollows

BEVIN BOY HERO

What did you do in the War, Grandad?
Why, I served my time as a Bevin Lad.
A lad, Grandad? But you'll be eighty next year.
True, I'm now much older, I fear.

One day, a letter fell on to the mat:
"Down the mine with you, boy" and that was that.
So off I went to do my bit
For King and Country in the pit.

And what did you find deep under the ground?
Coal, my boy, for that's where it's found.
Daily, we cut it, ton upon ton
Until at long last, the War was won.

Were you shot at, Grandad, in the mine?
No, but the roof caved in and I injured my spine.
Mum says you try but cannot walk.
Don't upset yourself, lad. That's woman's talk.

Well, who saved you, Grandad? Who rescued you then?
My friends, the miners, the bravest of men.
My life was their life and they risked their all
To dig me out from that dreadful fall.

Dad says you were called a "Forgotten Lad".
One of many, old chap but it wasn't all bad
For in darkness and dust, strong friendships grew
And I often think back to those heroes I knew.

You are not forgotten, Grandad, never, never.
I will remember you for ever and ever.
I am proud, so proud that you worked in the mine.
Goodnight and God bless you until the next time.

This poem is based on fact and is a tribute to an ex- Bevin Boy to whom I spoke recently. Buried by a heavy rock-fall, he sustained severe and disabling spinal injuries.
Despite his suffering, he remains stoical and shows great courage. He is a shining example to us all.

D. Hollows

A CHILLING PREDICTION

As my workmate, Charlie and I slithered and slid across the pit-yard to begin a new shift, we could not fail to notice a line of coal-laden wagons standing still and silent.

"Why aren't they moving?" I asked a passing deputy.

"Stuck to t'tracks, lad," came the reply. "Wi' snow like this it's a wonder owt's movin' at all."

For frozen, rigid fingers, even the heat of the oil-lamp was a welcome bonus. For a few minutes, it was a soothing and comforting sensation for this was the bitter Winter of 1947. Even the timbers sent to us underground were coated with thick ice and it took some time for the props to defrost in the warmth of the workings. Thank goodness ours was an upcast shaft at the bottom of which the furnace was situated. It was certainly preferable to labouring in the downcast shaft tunnels through which the pumped air passed. It is small wonder that so many descended wearing thick jackets, mufflers and even overcoats.

We Bevin Boys were still serving our country and awaiting demobilisation. There can be no doubting the fact that we would miss the companionship of our miner friends for they had been as father figures to us and had been instrumental in helping us emerge into manhood. However, it was gratifying to think that our days toiling in such harsh conditions were numbered.

The raw breeze stung our faces as we climbed the steps to the waiting banksman.

"Mornin', boys," he said. "Dead cold out theer, i'n't it? Let' s be 'a vin' you then. It's dreaded drop time again. I know you all 'ate it."

For the first time in two years, I felt a sense of eager anticipation at the thought of going underground once more.

"Hate it, hate it?" we chorused. "We're all looking forward to it."

"Wha's brought abaht this turnabout wi' you Bevin lads then?" queried Tom, the banksman.

"Look around," suggested Charlie.

"Can't see nowt save all that snow an' ice," came the reply.

"Well, there's your answer," Charlie smiled.

"Could be t'start of another Ice Age," Zak the collier added.

"If wha' tha's sayin' is reet," responded Tom "Next time tha comes up again, tha'll be a bunch o' owd fossils, frozen to t'marrer".

He gave the signal and down we went, mulling over his dismal prediction. We were young, somewhat gullible and a little apprehensive for the miner's opinion carried weight but all thoughts of our being solidified and transformed were dispelled with the ending of the cold snap.

Then, it was a return to, "Mornin', boys. Let's be 'avin' you then. It's dreaded drop time again. I know you all 'ate it," at which we nodded in assent.

WINTER 47

The pit-yard dressed in dappled white,
Shimmering, glowing in morning light.
Silent wagons bathed in sun
On coated tracks and loath to run.

Props encased in ice and snow,
Thawing, dripping down below:
Warmer there than here on top.
Will this cold spell ever stop?

"C'mon, lads, art ready to go?
In t'cage wi' thee an' don't be slow.
Mun be done for country an' Crown.
I know you boys 'ate goin' down".

"Hate it? Hate it?" we all said.
"Granted, it's comfy back in bed.
But we love it, love it, have no fear"
And in the cage we raised a cheer.

Banksman Tom then rang the bell,
Sending us on our way to Hell,
With single aim to stoke the fires,
As Tom mused, "Wha' a bunch o' ruddy liars."

D. Hollows

BROTHERS ALL

E. Bunting
Co. Durham Drift Mines

I am now 84 years of age and started work in 1938. I served throughout the War and afterwards and spent 27 years serving underground in drift mines, I was also a member of the Home Guard for 4 years and joined the organisation after twice running away to join the Royal Navy.

The Bevin Boys played a very important part in the history of Durham miners and mining. Some of them worked at our mine where we trained them and looked after them. My fellow workers and I struck up great friendships with the conscripts.
I remember one youngster who joined us. He responded well to the training and was fascinated by what went on in the mine and the conditions in which we worked. To say the least, they were terrible. In certain areas, the mine was very wet, the ventilation was poor and there were far more rats than workers.
One day, I turned up for the shift and found that my work- mate was missing. I imagined all sorts of things that might have happened to him but I needn't have bothered. He had packed

his bag and cleared off to Ireland. Looking back, I often think that he had more sense than the rest of us. The remainder of the Bevin Boys saw the War through.

They weren't a scrap of trouble and tried very hard in spite of the awful jobs they had to do.

HOMAGE

A chill wind blew as the old miner performed his daily ritual of visiting his old colliery. Stumbling along the path leading to the site, he wheezed from the legacy of deadly dust and paused to recover his breath. Before him lay muted dereliction where once there had been the sights and sounds of hectic activity. For so many years, that wasteland had been the focus of his working life and had enabled him to support his late wife and miner son whom Mother Nature had long claimed in the depths of the earth.

Staring at the sealed and abandoned ruin, he remembered his many friends of yesteryear. They had been as brothers, straining muscle and sinew to win the coal. In contemplation, he acknowledged the ignorance of the uninitiated who through no fault of their own making, were completely unaware of the hazards faced in those dark caverns. How little they knew of the many tragedies, of the becalming humour, especially during times of crisis, of the songs that echoed through the galleries and of the sheer relief felt as one emerged from the cage at the end of the shift.

As he reflected, a chronicle of events unfolded and memories came flooding back. He recalled the bleak days of the War when raw, young Bevin Boys had been committed to his charge and the freezing Winter of 1946 -1947 when laden wagons standing in the pit-yard were frozen to the tracks. He visualised the cold steel trams piled high with the spruce props and encased in an icy coating. For a brief moment, he glanced upward and imagined that he could see the flag of the N.C.B. fluttering in the breeze, heralding a new age for the miners, albeit a fleeting triumph.

With a final look, he turned and approached an adjoining field where once, the two pit ponies had run. It lay deserted and seemed forgotten in that backwater. But once, it had been enriched by the presence of little 'Pip', the Shetland and 'Tipper', the Exmoor. Together, they revelled in their new-found freedom and together, they would await his daily visits.

From afar, they could recognise him and their profound excitement was exhibited when they whinnied and galloped through the meadow to meet him. Often, he likened their display to those of the miners' children who would run to welcome their fathers and brothers from the mine.

Pip and Tipper would nuzzle him as he stroked their heads. He smiled to himself as he recalled their customary habit of exploring his coat pockets for their treats of apples, carrots and jam sandwiches. He loved them both dearly and knew that they responded in kind. It was thanks to Pip's obstinacy in refusing to move further down the haulage road that his life had been saved for had they proceeded, a massive roof-fall would have engulfed them both.

With a final pat and a kiss, he would leave them until the following day. Often, he gave thanks that they had been spared to see the daylight and to absorb the warmth of the sun's rays. Sadly, their reward had been all too brief for they were both long gone but he found solace in knowing that he had been chosen to share their lives. Instinctively and deep in thought, he reached out in a stroking motion, an action he had performed so often and in some strange way, he sensed that they were still there, nuzzling him, expectantly awaiting their treats. With tears in his-eyes, he waved at the emptiness before him, muttering, 'Be happy, dear friends' and slowly turned away.

Bending his head to the wind, he retraced his steps homeward and was filled with an overwhelming peace. God willing, he would repeat his pilgrimage the next day and for as long as he was able for that was the meaning of reverence. There would be so little to see but so much to feel. Now bereft of family and due to time's ceaseless rhythm, Pip, Tipper and his many mining friends, he considered himself truly blessed for he had a store of golden memories and he knew that he would never be alone.

D. Hollows

OPTION

Diane Ward
Gateshead

Option was given to the Wiseman family in April, 1971 for my cousin, Kate, to look after and ride. He came from a pit stables at Whiteoper, north of Newcastle-upon-Tyne and I believe that he came from either Blyth or Ellington.

He arrived with his tail and mane shaven and he was covered in coal dust. He was very muscular and when his hair grew again, he looked like a Shetland pony.

When the retired miners from the Bedlington Pit found that he had been rehomed, they made a point of visiting him in the field and in true mining tradition, offered him a variety of treats. They knew only too well that he was a retired pit pony.

I believe that it was customary at Option's colliery to name new arrivals in alphabetical order. Thus, he must have arrived at a time when the letter 'O' had been reached.

He was a much loved pet but eventually, Kate grew too big to ride him and in 1975, he went to live with a little girl in Bedlington. There, he lived for a further ten years and at the age of 40 years, he died of a heart attack.

He was a very intelligent pony as was frequently demonstrated when he decided to leave the field. He would open the gate by rubbing the latch with his rump until it opened. He could also squeeze himself through very narrow gaps despite his girth. I retain many happy memories of visiting my cousin and Option and going for long rides around the Bedlington countryside.

In the presence of family members, a young Diane sits on Option's back. The photograph was taken in 1973.
Diane, a retired school teacher, is a relative of the late Thomas (Tommy) Armstrong, the 'Pitman's Poet'.

THE NEWCASTLE CAT AND DOG SANCTUARY

Founded in 1896, the Newcastle Cat and Dog Shelter operates from two sites, Claremont Road and Benton North Farm. The shelters run at full capacity and at any one time, house up to 270 dogs and 200 cats. Every year, between 4,000 and 6,000 lost, unwanted, injured or neglected and abused animals are received. Both Centres are hives of activity.

When the Benton North Farm Sanctuary was opened, the staff inherited numerous farm animals, including Jersey cows, goats and sheep who live in lower field during the summer months and spend the winter months in the barn. All the farm animals take part in the Blessing of the Animals and Christmas Nativity Service which is held in conjunction with local schools.

Some years ago, Tony and Pike, two retired pit ponies from Ellington Colliery, arrived at the centre and together, they revelled in their new-found freedom. Sadly, Pike passed away in May, 2005 and Tony has now been befriended by Willie, a black Shetland pony who as a foal, was donated to the sanctuary by a local vicar. Both ponies can often be heard neighing to each other and to the visitors from their summer field behind the farm house.

Members of staff face their daunting task with dedication and compassion. Among them, are volunteers whose love of animals translates words into deeds and their reward lies in re-establishing their charges into happy, stable and caring homes. The Shelters do not receive any government funding and rely entirely on donations and legacies from members of the public. Fund-raising events are ongoing and there are so many ways in which one can support the Sanctuaries.

For further information, please contact:

Newcastle Dog and Cat Shelter,
Benton North Farm,
Benton Lane,
Newcastle upon Tyne,
NE12 8EH, Tel. 0191 215 0435

Reg. Charity No. 220506
Website: www.dogandcatshelter.com

PIKE AT ELLINGTON COLLIERY

Pike thoroughly enjoyed his retirement and loved to greet visitors to his paddock.

THE BEST OF FRIENDS

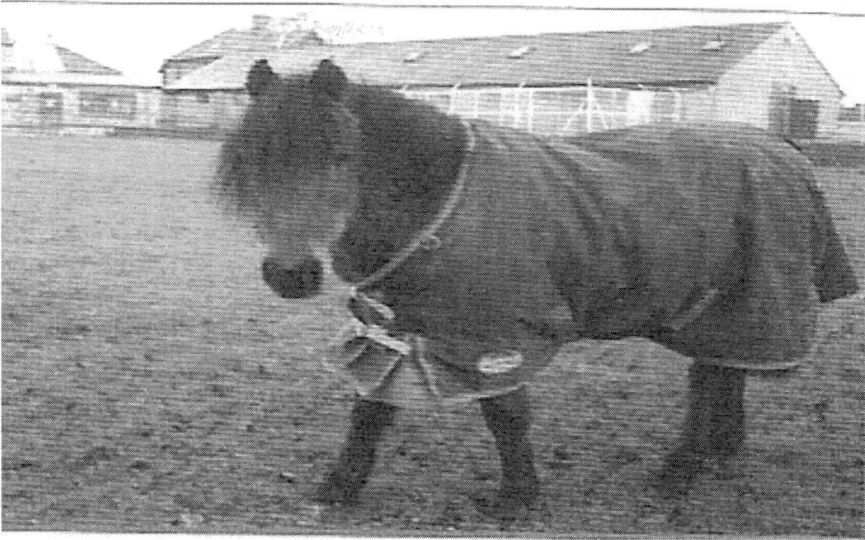

TONY

WILLIE

CAUSE FOR CONCERN

A very moving article on the subject of pit ponies was published in the 19th October, 1997 issue of the "People" newspaper and extracts are here reproduced by kind permission of journalist, Alexandra Williams and the said newspaper.

"A flicker of light breaking the black sheet of darkness is followed by a low rumbling and the sound of splashing water.
Gradually, the daylight picks different shapes and pieces together the form emerging from the mine - a pony blackened by coal, his ears clogged with dust.
He snorts heavily. Black fumes billow from his nostrils and his strained head moves up and down. Steam rolls off his belly. His hooves squelch through the black mud as he negotiates the flooded tramlines and debris.
A metal harness encases his body and attached at the back is a battered tram laden with a ton of coal - the equivalent weight of a rhinoceros and heavier than a car. This is Patch, a pit pony. And this is 1997. Like a robot programmed to perform, he dutifully trudges to the tipping point.
Patch is unhooked and without instruction, walks to the other end of the tram. He has done this hundreds of times.
Once it has been tipped on to the grading sieve, the tram is

attached to his harness and he resumes his journey to the depths.

Only the ugly plastic tubing pumping fresh air into the mine ruined the illusion that this was a scene from the turn of the century.

Incredibly, shockingly, Patch is not unique. Britain, a leader in technology, still has working pit ponies.

Their cheapness - you can pick one up for £200 to £300 from a traveller or at the local market - coupled with their reliability make them perfect mine machinery. And there's always a buyer once the pony is past it - they fetch 50p a pound for dog meat.

The latest legislation relating to pit ponies, first used in the 1770's, was drawn up in 1956. Since then there has been nothing.

No government body solely concerned with the welfare of the animals makes regular visits to the mines. It is left, by and large, to the mine owner. He decides how long the pony will work . He decides how much is loaded into the tram and he decides where the pony sleeps.

A Health and Safety Executive spokesman admitted that the mine's inspectors' main concern is the welfare of the workers.

'Our inspectors will take a look at the horses when they're visiting a mine and if they have any doubts about their welfare they'll invite a vet to check it over', he said.

The inspectors don't have any qualifications to do with animals but they're the only people around to do an independent check.

The use of pit ponies was only brought to the attention of the British Horse Society last Spring. The R.S.P.C.A. knew nothing about it until 1992."

THE HORSE AND PONY CENTRE & PIT PONY CENTRE

Angela and Roy opened their sanctuary in 1988 when they purchased a farm where they could care for needy horses and ponies. Their burning ambition was expressed thus: "One day, there will be a secure home for the Welsh pit ponies and other needy horses and ponies in Wales. It will be a large grassland farm with a good range of buildings for old bones on cold, winter nights, mature trees to shade them from the mid-day sun, a natural spring feeding a babbling brook to drink long and cool from on hot summer days. It will be accessible by road and public transport with good facilities for all people to enjoy meeting the ponies. Here, they will forget their previous harsh life and enjoy their well-earned retirement for the rest of their days."

Over the years, they have rescued a number of animals whose lives were blighted by drudgery and in certain cases, ill-treatment. Currently, they care for 26 horses and ponies and with the help, of dedicated staff, they do their utmost to provide a supportive environment for their charges which should be the right of all creatures. Among them, are some pit ponies who have spent their working lives in the darkness and choking dust of the mine. It is small wonder that they now suffer from lung diseases and other complaints.

Steel is a case in point. He retired to the Centre in 1998. Sold as a five year old, he was taken underground where he was used to haul laden tubs from the coal-face to the surface. Sadly, his breathing is now impaired. However, on the positive side and because of the tender care that he has received, he revels in his new- found freedom.

As with many other animals, Steel's story is very moving and his multifarious experiences of hardship and deprivation would fill a book. When rescued, his pink flesh and rolls of muscle were permeated with thick layers of coal dust and there were bald patches where his harness had been worn. He was in a poor physical condition which was confirmed by a vet, who examined him. Thanks to the staff at the Sanctuary, his health began to improve, albeit slowly. That is but one part of Steel's biography, the poignant yet triumphant tale of a pit pony reborn and restored to happiness.

There are countless creatures who continue to lead wretched lives because of man's negligence and indifference to their basic needs. It is reassuring to know that Angela, Roy and an army of concerned members of the public transform sentiment into positive action. Through them, a ray of hope emerges from the darkness of despair and they are so deserving of our full support.

Charity No. 1002933
Fforest Uchaf Horse and Pony Centre
& The Pit Pony Sanctuary,
Penycoedcae,
Pontypridd,
Rhondda Cynon Taff,
CF37 IPS.
Tel. 01443 480327

www.pitponies.co.uk
www.sponsorapony.co.uk
www.unusualanduniquegift.com
www.pitponies.co.uk/storysteel.htm

Details of open dates and times are available from the Centre.

Steel (right) and friend, Jake. They play hard together until Steel starts to struggle for breath

Steel's stable before he was rescued

Pit pony Bob meets Her Majesty, Queen Elizabeth in 2000.
Recently, Bob passed away peacefully in his stable

Bob working at the mine, 1997

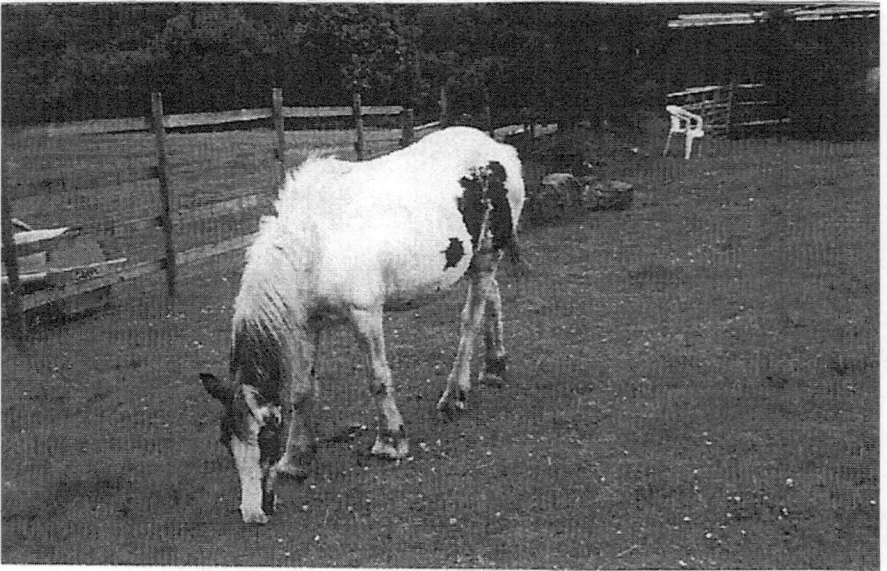

Bob at the Sanctuary 2006

Buttons found dumped in a field

AS IT SHOULD BE

The Sanctuary's success story but there still remains so much to do and so many animals to be rescued.

SLAVES OF THE LONG NIGHT

Deep in the bowels of that black abode,
in passageways hewn from the rigid rock,
Time is an enigma ignored by the clock,
where each must carry his own heavy load.

Here, there is no dusk and there is no dawn.
Time as always, unaltering remains,
one long night harnessed to these leafless lanes.
No songbird sings and no new day is born.

Blind pit ponies, slaves of that long night:
for these poor creatures, no pastures green,
no field of flowers will ever be seen,
white-eyed in the darkness, craving the light.

Blinking in the haulier's lamp-lit glare,
the rough-clad timbers groaning overhead,
as with bleeding fetlocks, they stumble tread
along that never-ending circuit where

Danger is as constant as the choking dust
and whilst they struggle on deep down below,
high above, Springtime erupts to flow
in a rapturous feeling of lush green lust.

J. Anthony Rock

GLOSSARY

(Relevant Lancashire dialect terms)

ain't	is not, are not
all but	almost, nearly
allus	always
didna	did not, didn't you?
gie o'er	give over, stop, you're kidding
gorra	got a
gorrit	got it
leckie	battery-operated lamp affixed to safety-helmet
like tha'	like that
mun	must
mun't	must not
neet	night
nowt	nothing
owd	old
pigtail	chewing tobacco
plug	piece of pigtail
reet	right
sin'	since
sithee	see you, look here (depending on context)
snap	lunch
summat	something
tha, thee	you
thowt	thought
thine	yours
thysen	yourself
toneet	tonight
weer	where
why ar't?	why are you?
wom	home

RELEVANT TECHNICAL TERMS

backings   saddle chains

bank   surface

banksman   official in charge of pit-head

braffin   horse's/pony's collar filled with straw

chum   empty tub

chummings   set of tubs

driver   miner in charge of pony engaged on haulage work

fulluns   full tubs

hewer   collier/coal winner

in-bye   toward the workings

limbers   pony's haulage apparatus. Short shafts into which pony was guided to pull tubs. A yoke, fastened to the pony's sides by ridge chain and rump straps. The shafts were joined at rear by an iron fitting and attached by a steel pin to a lug on the tub

longwall   system in which two parallel roadways are driven at right angles to the coal-face which may be several hundred metres long. As the face advances, the waste is used to pack the rear areas. The roof is then collapsed thus taking the weight from the coal-face. A safety measure

on-setter   man in charge at bottom of shaft

out-bye   away from the workings

overman   another name for a deputy

pullings   collar chains

putter   usually a piece-worker using a pony for haulage

tailgate   heading off main haulage way

timber leader   miner responsible for delivering timber wherever required

trace chain   chain used when pony pulling load up gradient end chains

trappings   end chains

The glossary of dialect and technical terms is limited solely to those included in this book. There are many variations throughout the coalfields.

INDEX